PRAISE FOR *LIFT*

"Leadership is no longer an exclusive role held by few, as discussed in *Lift*, but instead is a position that requires compassionate flexibility, collaboration, and confidence. With constant societal, environmental, and professional changes in our world, transactional leadership just won't cut it anymore."

—JENNIFER EGGERS, founder and president of Leader*Shift* Insights Inc. and author of the international best seller *Resilience: It's Not About Bouncing Back*

"What will it take to lead in this Fourth Industrial Revolution? Between pandemics, climate change, social unrest, AI, and new technologies, the only normal in the 'new normal' is constant change. In his compelling new book, Faisal Hoque gives a much-needed *Lift* to leaders who want to stay on the forefront of change, and not be left behind."

—ALAIN HUNKINS, CEO of Hunkins Leadership Group and author of *Cracking the Leadership Code: Three Secrets to Building Strong Leaders*

"In this century, we are experiencing global challenges that require transformative leadership in order to mitigate impending disasters. This book outlines the challenges we face in the modern world and how leaders will need to address them."

—RONALD E. RIGGIO, PHD, Henry R. Kravis professor of leadership and organizational psychology, Claremont McKenna College, Kravis Leadership Institute

"Transformational leadership takes a good deal of learning and becoming better every day, far beyond good intentions. In his insightful and practical book, *Lift*, Faisal Hoque shares great lessons beyond the realms of the Fourth Industrial Revolution. I highly recommend *Lift* to all leaders aiming to enhance their leadership capacity for growth and crafting their own lives embracing a brighter future for others."

—DR. OLEG KONOVALOV, one of the top global leaders on leadership and author of *The Vision Code*, the da Vinci of visionary leadership

"An inspiring book that helps us to be aware of the huge world changes and our role as leaders in different contexts. Faisal Hoque highlights the importance of enhancing our human skills and empathy as leaders in a world increasingly automated due to the Fourth Industrial Revolution. The author includes in his discussion the complex times that came along with the pandemic and its effects on our lifestyle. This book is friendly to read and has a didactic structure, which makes it valuable not only for scholars but also practitioners, managers, entrepreneurs, and anyone that wants to lead successfully in this complex environment that we live in."

—FRANCOISE CONTRERAS, PHD, profesor de la Universidad del Rosario.

"The leadership dynamic experienced a seismic shift during COVID that requires a new approach to empower an organization. In *Lift*, Faisal Hoque offers innovative steps on transformational leadership that demonstrates how empathy is a crucial aspect in inspiring higher levels of organizational effectiveness."

—ERIK NELSON, senior vice president of CACI International, Inc.

"*Lift* is itself an act of transformational leadership. Faisal Hoque guides us with wisdom, empathy, and optimism through the complex, confusing—and often frightening—convergent forces at work which are changing the way we interact with our communities and our entire biosphere. Hoque leads us through the deep work necessary to recognize the import of those sweeping changes and urges us to take pragmatic action to become an agent for positive change—the kind of person who can transform good intentions into leading others to meaningful action and positive impact. Our children, and their children, may one day ask about these times, 'What were you thinking? What were you doing?' If you are asking yourself, 'What can I do?' this book is for you. Faisal Hoque gives us clarity, purpose, direction—and hope."

—G. SHAWN HUNTER, CEO of Mindscaling and author of *Small Acts of Leadership*

"Amid the tumult of change we are experiencing comes *Lift* by Faisal Hoque. This book diagnoses what's going wrong and provides insight into what leaders can do to improve the situation for all of us. Backed by research, coupled with compelling narratives, Hoque delivers a path forward that we want to embrace because it is doable now."

—JOHN BALDONI, executive coach at Global Guru/Leadership, and author of fifteen books, including *Grace Notes: Leading in an Upside-Down World*

"Transformational leadership is a daily practice meant for all. Bravo, Faisal Hoque, for going beyond leadership theory and expertly providing actionable steps for the aspiring leader."

—MERETE WEDELL-WEDELLSBORG, professor of leadership at IMD Business School and author of *Battle Mind: How to Navigate in Chaos* and *Perform Under Pressure*

LIFT

FOSTERING THE LEADER IN YOU
AMID REVOLUTIONARY GLOBAL CHANGE

FAISAL HOQUE

WITH JEFF WUORIO AND SHELLEY MOENCH-KELLY

FAST
COMPANY
Press

Fast Company Press
New York, New York
www.fastcompanypress.com

This work is being published under the Fast Company Press imprint by an exclusive arrangement with *Fast Company*. *Fast Company* and the *Fast Company* logo are registered trademarks of Mansueto Ventures, LLC. The Fast Company Press logo is a wholly owned trademark of Mansueto Ventures, LLC.

Distributed by Greenleaf Book Group

For ordering information or special discounts for bulk purchases, please contact Greenleaf Book Group at PO Box 91869, Austin, TX 78709, 512.891.6100.

Design and composition by Greenleaf Book Group and Sheila Parr
Cover design by Greenleaf Book Group and Sheila Parr

Publisher's Cataloging-in-Publication data is available.

Print ISBN: 978-1-63908-012-0

eBook ISBN: 978-1-63908-013-7

Part of the Tree Neutral® program, which offsets the number of trees consumed in the production and printing of this book by taking proactive steps, such as planting trees in direct proportion to the number of trees used: www.treeneutral.com

TreeNeutral®

Printed in the United States of America on acid-free paper

22 23 24 25 26 27 28 29   10 9 8 7 6 5 4 3 2 1

First Edition

To Rian,

In a world full of turbulence, you have been the light that keeps me going . . .
From the moment you were born, you have inspired me to be my better self.
I am in awe of your courage, composure, attitude, resilience—
leadership traits every one of us should be striving for.

This is for you and the readers . . .
May you all thrive with beauty, happiness, and strength.

*"Let us not pray to be sheltered from dangers
but to be fearless when facing them."*
—*Rabindranath Tagore*

CONTENTS

INTRODUCTION

IN A WORLD BEING TRANSFORMED by unprecedented change, effective, meaningful leadership is becoming even more essential.

That offers historic opportunities, provided we recognize the type of leaders we need to have and what those leaders need to do to carry out a different form of leadership.

Sweeping change is everywhere, much of it focused on technology. Labeled the "Fourth Industrial Revolution (4IR)," emerging technologies and their interactions with one another are upending how we work, play, educate, and govern ourselves. Artificial intelligence, augmented reality, big data, multidimensional printing, and the development of varied collaborative tools such as "cobots"—robots designed to interact physically with human beings in a collaborative environment—are just a sampling of the power and pervasiveness of technological disruption.

But 4IR is not only about smart, connected machines and systems. Its scope is much wider as well. For instance, waves of further breakthroughs are happening at the same time in areas ranging from gene sequencing to nanotechnology to quantum computing.

It is the fusion of these technologies and their interactions across the physical, digital, and biological domains that is transforming how we work, play, live, and communicate. As Klaus Schwab, executive chairman of the World Economic Forum, notes, this change promises to transform our very identities: "The Fourth Industrial Revolution, finally, will change not only what we do but also who we are. It will affect our identity and all the issues associated with it: our sense of privacy, our notions of ownership, our consumption patterns, the time we devote to work and leisure, and how we develop our careers, cultivate our skills, meet people, and nurture relationships."[1]

However, while many may focus exclusively on this explosion of technology, the Fourth Industrial Revolution is by no means the sole driver of worldwide change. Rather, something of a perfect storm of factors is powering this level of sweeping disruption.

The COVID-19 pandemic has and will continue to change many of the fundamental aspects of how we live our lives. As we are forced to adjust and redo how we work, socialize, take care of ourselves, and educate our children, the practical and psychological effects of the pandemic will continue to impact us all—as consumers, businesspeople, students, and citizens. In many respects, the changes wrought by COVID-19 will by no means disappear once the virus and its derivatives are safely brought under control.

Long an issue eliciting varied degrees of concern, climate change has also emerged as a major force of disruption. Although perhaps the most visible and prominent result lies in a growing number of environmental disasters—the recent severe winter weather in the southern United States being one such example—climate change is also upending our choices as consumers, who are prioritizing environmental impact and product durability, and shopping at a local level whenever possible. Business models now need to take green policies into consideration and make them visible to and understandable by the public. Government is now more than ever compelled to address pollution, traffic, and the impact of development at all levels—as a more informed and connected citizenry is paying attention.

An additional, insidious driver of change is misinformation. Disseminated and reinforced by social media, twisted truths and outright lies are leading us to question not only who to believe and why but also our confidence in health care, government, education, public discourse, and other bedrocks of society that up until recently went largely unchallenged.

This tsunami of change and disruption carries enormous consequences. It also carries unprecedented responsibilities. The faster most everything changes and the greater the level of disruption, the faster we all need to learn how to direct that change.

And when I say all of us, I mean *all* of us.

Such a broad seismic shift has effectively empowered every person, group, and organization to be leaders in widely varying capacities. Individual access to data and connectivity—coupled with varied forces that have reworked how we see ourselves and the world around us—have catalyzed and made possible the opportunity to participate, contribute, and influence at unprecedented levels in most every aspect of life. In varied ways, we have all become leaders.

But not just any type of leader.

Traditionally, leaders operated in a transactional environment—a hierarchical system primarily focused on short-term results. The basic procedure was straightforward:

- A leader handed down directions.

- From there, the leader monitored results and performance— sometimes, perhaps too closely.

- The leader rewarded good performance—usually, monetarily— and punished poor performance.

- The cycle was repeated ad infinitum.

That's not to suggest that everything about transactional leadership is bad. After all, it only makes sense to incentivize good work and discourage the substandard. Rather, it's more an issue as to what transactional leadership is *not* designed to do that makes it ill-suited to a world characterized by change.

For one thing, transactional leadership's emphasis on the short term isn't positioned to foster long-term thinking and planning. When dynamic change can quickly transform what's current to outdated, vision that goes beyond tomorrow is essential to recognize the change that's occurring and how to plan and act to best leverage that change over an extended time frame.

Transactional leadership is also geared to fixed, rigid processes: "Do it this way and be rewarded accordingly." Urging others to just "stick to the script" effectively discourages creativity and innovation—two attributes that will prove essential to constantly adapting to how we work, live, play, and learn. Old solutions derived from conventional thinking and action will prove largely useless.

The far more effective alternative is transformational leadership. The concept of transformational leadership started with James V. Downton in 1973 and was expanded by James Burns in 1978. In 1985, researcher Bernard M. Bass further expanded the concept to include ways for measuring the success of transformational leadership. There are four factors to transformational leadership, also known as the "Four I's": idealized influence, inspirational motivation, intellectual stimulation, and individual consideration.

Transformational leaders focus on *people*—they encourage, inspire, and motivate those around them to innovate and foster positive change. These leaders encourage autonomy and creativity. They are open and responsive to change. They're agile by choice, not by mandate.

They are keenly aware of the impact their decisions have on those around them, as well as themselves. Transformational leaders understand that their values and integrity embodied in their actions and choices are both internal *and* external models. How they choose to lead themselves works hand in hand with how they work with and inspire others.

In a world of explosive change and transformation, transformational leadership at all levels—from heads of state down to individuals—offers the best opportunity to leverage change to transform all our lives for the better. That goes for how we work, play, govern ourselves, and consider and plan for our collective future.

But acquiring and becoming skillful at the characteristics of transformational leadership takes a good deal more than good intentions. As was touched on earlier, transformational leadership comes from a conscious, consistent practice of empathy. To truly empower others to be their very best, a transformational leader must be aware not only of their abilities but also of their weaker characteristics—that, and have a supportive attitude toward overcoming those challenges. The future will mandate true collaboration and cooperation, attributes that can only be achieved with leadership that's as fully in touch as possible.

But the environment in which we find ourselves calls for more than just understanding that a new style of leadership affords the best opportunity to leverage change for the common good. It's just as necessary to know how to execute that leadership style in real-world circumstances. Sustainable impact derives from both systemic thinking and execution. Empathy in and of itself is a praiseworthy element of transformational leadership. But lacking a thoughtful, empirical means with which to put transformational leadership into practical action leaves it as just that—good intentions.

All that begs the question—if empathy and systemic execution are so essential to leveraging an environment of exponential change, where do you go to learn those and other skills of transformational leadership? The answer is *experiential learning*. As you'll see later in this book, education in all its varied forms will benefit by shifting a greater emphasis toward experiential learning—from grade school to college and beyond that, with an ongoing focus on acquiring meaningful, relevant skills. Not only has experiential learning proven highly successful in the past in terms of student engagement and other measures, but it's also the most effective way to learn in a world where so much is changing so fast. The lessons of 12 hours ago—let alone days or weeks—are often yesterday's news. The more immersive and ongoing the learning, the more useful and applicable the end results.

Experiential learning will also prove essential outside a classroom setting. As leaders scramble to cope with effective means to promote and carry out successful leadership—particularly transformational leadership—learning on the fly from what we experience will be critical to evaluating and adapting to a world in exponential flux. The new book of the "rules" of leadership is being written and rewritten constantly—experiential learning affords the best opportunity to keep pace with that seemingly incessant change.

That this level of extraordinary change we're experiencing can seriously backfire against us has already been shown. The horrific, unprecedented events of the violent uprising in Washington, DC, on January 6, 2021, underscore that very real danger—a threat that Stanford law professor Nathaniel Persily foreshadowed in a 2019 report, *The Internet's Challenge to Democracy: Framing the Problem and Assessing Reforms*, where Persily points out that the "original promise of digital technologies was unapologetically democratic. . . . That promise has been replaced by concern that the most democratic features of the internet are, in fact, endangering democracy itself. Democracies pay a price for internet freedom, under this view, in the form of disinformation, hate speech, incitement, and foreign interference in elections."[2]

That example from public events underscores a call to action for leadership—for government, obviously, but also the technology industry's complicity in providing a platform for dissemination of perilous disinformation that threatened the physical safety of our nation's leaders, literally.

But it's also a call to action for every one of us as leaders—leaders who recognize our own responsibility to identify and mitigate the spread and import of feigned information directed toward destruction. That applies to individuals, as well as business leaders, community groups, educators, the religious community—all leaders empowered to make a difference.

But issues such as misinformation are not merely problems to be addressed. They're also enormous opportunities that afford the chance not just to right wrongs but also to build something far better in their place. The dichotomy of danger/reward exists throughout the upheaval of change we're experiencing. For instance, climate change is undeniably perilous, but it's also been called the greatest health-care opportunity of the 21st century.

How each of us act as leaders will dictate whether the outcome will be outright disaster or a healthy, ecologically stable planet. That's one reason this book has a one-word primary title. When we talk about "lift," it refers to the opportunity we all have to contribute to the betterment of everyone through transformational leadership. We may act individually, but the impact of what each of us does can be truly global.

The opportunity that transformational leadership offers the leader in everyone is both significant and meaningful. We all have an obligation to ourselves and others to understand, nurture, and manage the "revolution" that's taking place—rather than having revolutionary change manage us. That will mandate the right kind of leadership skills be systematically developed and implemented, open to ongoing change and adjustment to react to the reinvention that is mostly everywhere.

HOW THIS BOOK IS ARRANGED

Change and disruption of the magnitude we're experiencing call for a response that isn't mere wishful thinking, a spirited prayer hoping for the best. Rather, it requires both substance and strategy—that we all are fast becoming leaders in varied capacities and that the resulting evolution mandates a leadership style geared to the level and speed of the change that's taking hold at an ever-increasing rate.

The book is divided into three different sections. The first, titled "Where We Are Now," encompasses four chapters, each of which examines the four drivers of revolutionary change we're experiencing—the Fourth Industrial Revolution, COVID-19, climate change, and pervasive misinformation. Each chapter will address each driver's impact on a variety of areas, including work, education, health care, government, and the individual. How have these four factors transformed how we see ourselves, others, and the varied groups and institutions that compose society? Moreover, how unlikely is it that we will revert back to habits, routines, practices, and beliefs that once were considered sacrosanct?

The second section, "Amid the Change, All This Opportunity," will offer a detailed examination of the various opportunities that the level of change we're experiencing affords all of us—as consumers, workers, educators, and individual members of an increasingly connected society. More flexible, engaging work; cost-effective health care; practical and affordable education; connected and responsive government—these are just a sampling of the many opportunities sweeping change has made possible.

But only if it's managed properly and proactively. The final section, titled "Be Transformational," will examine the components of transformational leadership, how such a leadership style is best positioned to direct change, and what specifically every one of us as individual transformational leaders needs to do to best involve ourselves to leverage change to achieve the utmost good. Here, the importance of execution is reinforced—the imperative of systematically putting transformational leadership into action, bridging the more emotional elements of leadership with pragmatic application.

Each chapter will include a variety of sidebars, most of which are personal anecdotes and observations from this book's three authors and other professional colleagues. In these, we'll share stories, recollections, and ideas detailing how we've all experienced the changes that this book examines. They're also an important element of transformational leadership. By sharing relatable stories and thoughts, we look to display a genuine sense of empathy with readers. It's a quiet reminder that we're all in this challenging environment together—the more we can all learn from each other, the more successful we can become as leaders in our own right.

To further the value and use of this book, included at the end of every chapter is a section titled "Learn and Transform." Culled from material from each chapter, this feature will offer pertinent, actionable suggestions and guidance that you can use to put the principles in this book into meaningful action—the sort of experiential learning that can produce transformational leaders with the skills to enact lasting, beneficial change.

SECTION ONE

WHERE WE ARE NOW

CHAPTER 1

THE FOURTH INDUSTRIAL REVOLUTION

FOR SOMETHING THAT'S AS IMPACTFUL and far-reaching in its ramifications, the Fourth Industrial Revolution—also known as "4IR"—can seem rather "fuzzy" to many.

That's because the optimal term often associated with this explosion—"event" seems inadequate to capture it—is blurry. Unlike more autonomous forms of disruption and transformation, the Fourth Industrial Revolution is blurring the lines that historically separated physical, biological, and digital arenas. Easy compartmentalization is no longer the rule.

As with its predecessors, the Fourth Industrial Revolution marks a continuation of the disruption that preceded it. Leveraging power generated through water and steam, the First Industrial Revolution introduced mechanized production. The Second employed electric power to create mass production. The Third used electronics and information technology to automate production.

Now a Fourth Industrial Revolution is building on the Third: the digital revolution that has been occurring since the middle of the last century. But rather than focusing just on digital growth, 4IR is driven largely by the convergence of digital, biological, and physical innovations. The rise of artificial intelligence (AI), robotics, the Internet of Things (IoT), autonomous vehicles, 3D printing, nanotechnology, biotechnology, and quantum computing are all elements of this massive union of technology and accessibility.

But the fourth iteration differs from the prior revolutions in a number of other meaningful, impactful ways. Perhaps most distinctive, as well as significant, is the exponential speed with which change and disruption is occurring. Given that so much of that change is focused on technological innovation and implementation, which, in turn, fuels and drives change in other areas, the momentum of 4IR essentially nurtures itself, accelerating both the speed of disruption and the scope of its import.

Evolving and exploding technology unto itself underscores the depth of 4IR's impact. A mere sampling of that technology includes the following:

- **Artificial intelligence (AI).** AI is one of the cornerstones of change. It is defined as the ability of a digital computer or computer-controlled robot to carry out tasks generally performed by humans, and one of its most telling characteristics is its capacity to learn. Its appeal is widespread. As of this writing, 90 percent of leading businesses have ongoing investments in varied AI technologies.[1]

- **Internet of Things (IoT).** This connection between digital and physical environments means more than just the capacity of kitchen appliances to "speak" to one another or connected individual health monitors that track blood pressure, glucose levels, and other health data. As Kevin Ashton, the British technology pioneer who cofounded the Auto-ID Center at the Massachusetts Institute of Technology, noted some years ago, the IoT is capable of gathering information on its own and, from there, acting on that data: "Often what it does with that information is not tell a human being something, it [just] does something."[2] Another example of the IoT "just doing something" rather than offering advice or guidance is used every day by millions of travelers—a hotel key or, rather, a mobile device armed with the technology to open guest rooms without the need for an additional plastic card or, even more outdated, an actual physical key. These devices can also be used for other purposes, such as notifying guests of events of interest and managing room service orders.

- **Cobots.** These are a more mature iteration of robots designed to interact physically with humans collaboratively. Much of the focus of their use will fall on a wide range of industrial applications, particularly in repetitive jobs such as assembly, material handling, and other tasks potentially dangerous to human workers. Cobots will also work in more consumer-oriented settings. For instance, in mid-2021, America's Domino's pizza chain debuted a pizza delivery robot car in the Houston area.[3] The first completely autonomous, human-free, on-road delivery vehicle to receive regulatory approval from the United States Department of Transportation, the car allows customers to receive texts with updates on its location and offers a numerical code that can be used to retrieve the order once the car arrives. Elsewhere, Chinese tech company Baidu introduced a driverless taxi service in 2021, making it the first such one in China.[4]

Fig. 1.1. Photo by Andy Kelly on Unsplash.

- **Big data.** A tsunami of data is of little use unless it can be massaged into useful information. Big data will drive that change, producing practical information for everything from business to governmental policy. In particular, quantum computing's capacity to examine and analyze complicated information much faster than conventional computers will contribute significantly to the effective management and use of enormous stores of data.

- **Multidimensional printing.** Whether 3D or 4D printing, this exploding technology is revolutionizing prototype development in architecture, mechanical engineering, urban planning, and other applications. This area is forecast to grow exponentially in the coming years as market options increase and use of blended materials becomes more readily available.

A GROWING NUMBER OF "CONNECTIONS"

More and more, we're finding ourselves standing at the intersection of humanity and technology. Whether we're working side by side with autonomous robots on the factory floor, spreading the happy news about a new addition to the family on Facebook, or asking Siri to help us get from point A to point B as quickly as possible, all aspects of our lives are closely connected to technology in one way or another.

Some of those "connections" can be downright threatening. "The Fourth Industrial Revolution, which includes developments in previously disjointed fields such as artificial intelligence (AI), machine-learning, robotics, nanotechnology, 3-D printing, and genetics and biotechnology," is expected "to cause widespread disruption not only to business models but also to labor markets over the next five years," the World Economic Forum reports, with "enormous change predicted in the skill sets needed to thrive in the new landscape."[5]

According to a 2017 University of Oxford study, developed nations can expect to see job loss rates of up to 47 percent within the next 25 years. Additionally, a Pew Research Center study found that "robotics and artificial intelligence will permeate wide segments of daily life by 2025, with huge implications for a range of industries such as healthcare, transport and logistics, customer service, and home maintenance."[6]

Most of us are increasingly unprepared for this rapidly changing world of working. Should we all focus on enhancing our technical skills? What about those so-called soft skills, such as critical thinking, communication, empathy, mindfulness, resiliency, decision-making, self-awareness, and so forth, that make us better leaders?

In this era of technology and automation, where news articles foreshadow a time when robots will take over our jobs, technology vendors churn out new innovations on an almost-daily basis, and companies scramble to find alternative sources of labor, where do the humanities stand?

continued

In my view, the skills that come from a strong education in the humanities are becoming more important than ever.

A recent Royal Bank of Canada research paper, "Humans Wanted—How Canadian Youth Can Thrive in the Age of Disruption," found the following:[7]

- Being "human" will ensure resiliency in an era of disruption and artificial intelligence.

- Skills mobility—the ability to move from one job to another—will become a new competitive advantage.

- The demand for "human skills" will grow across all job sectors and will include critical thinking, coordination, social perceptiveness, active listening, and complex problem-solving.

- Rather than a nation of coders, digital literacy—the ability to understand digital items, digital technologies, or the internet fluently—will be necessary for all new jobs.

- Global competencies such as cultural awareness, language, and adaptability will be in demand. Virtually all job openings will place significant importance on judgment and decision-making, and more than two-thirds will value an ability to manage people and resources.

In his book *You Can Do Anything: The Surprising Power of a "Useless" Liberal Arts Education*, George Anders says, "Curiosity, creativity, and empathy aren't unruly traits that must be reined in. You can be yourself, as an English major, and thrive in sales. You can segue from anthropology into the booming new field of user research; from classics into management consulting; and from philosophy into high-stakes investing. You can bring a humanist's grace to our rapidly evolving high-tech future. And if you know how to attack the job market, your opportunities will be vast."[8]

When I was a kid, I wanted to become an entrepreneur, engineer, and inventor. And I have been passionately pursuing that dream since then. What I did not realize then is how much personal gratification I would get from writing. Writing is one of those happy discoveries that has helped me to connect better with my purpose, myself, and

THE FOURTH INDUSTRIAL REVOLUTION

my career goals. Writing has allowed me to find myself when I was looking for answers. The ability to write is a critical human skill.

I knew at the very beginning of my career in the early '90s that technology would have a serious impact on socioeconomic growth, individually and organizationally.

What I had to learn is that there is a dividing line where automation ends, and basic humanities (or so-called soft skills) have to step up to the plate. Even Tesla's Elon Musk admits that over-automation has hampered creativity and productivity at his company, which is well known for its innovative, out-of-the-box thinking on the automobile-manufacturing front. In other words, where human interaction ends and full automation begins, ideas can die—maybe never to come back.

The constant cascade of new technologies will continue to create a more empowered population. We will be increasingly connected and isolated at the same time. We will demand more self-expressions. Within this topsy-turvy context, we all will have to learn how to leverage humanities to connect, inspire, and influence others and ourselves. It will be our collective responsibility to realize that humans can't be replaced by technology; we have to ensure exactly how the two will intersect and intertwine in our future world.

—Faisal Hoque

The Fourth Industrial Revolution, however, takes in more than all sorts of new technology coming into play at an ever-faster rate. This enormous confluence of new tools and technology has impacted most every element of how we live our lives. In one respect, this—along with the effects of the COVID-19 pandemic—has fostered an explosion of remote work. Although the necessity of distance and isolation due to the pandemic has driven the increase in remote work—according to a survey by Gartner Inc., 88 percent of organizations worldwide mandated or encouraged their employees to work from home after COVID-19 was declared a pandemic—a surge in availability and use of remote collaboration devices,

EARLY SIGNS
OF CHANGE

It was roughly in 2015 that I noticed the business world around me changing. Prior to that, we relied solely on email, phone, or in-person interactions to communicate with one another. Slowly, applications including Skype, Trello, Slack, and Zoom became the platforms du jour in our daily operations. The last CEO I worked for refused to learn these revolutionary methods of connecting and was eventually replaced by the board of directors, who saw her attitude as disturbing—as someone who might also refuse to help grow the company. That's how tuned in they were. Looking back, I almost don't remember the times before these applications existed. They—among many other technological discoveries— have truly served to connect everyone on the planet regardless of location or time zone.

—Shelley Moench-Kelly

such as video streaming, application and desktop sharing, and other similar capabilities, has allowed for remote work at unprecedented levels. Put another way, the technology was always coming. The pandemic merely pushed its emergence into a higher gear.[9]

Nor is this a trend that seems destined to decline once COVID-19 is brought under control, in many observers' eyes. According to a study by the University of Southern California's Center for the Digital Future, 30 percent of Americans say that even if they could go back to work safely, they don't want to.[10] A growing number of companies, particularly in technology fields, have announced they're going to allow their employees to work from home after the pandemic. For instance, music provider Spotify announced in February 2021 that it will allow its entire staff to work from remote locations permanently.[11] How that is planned and implemented with a sense of balance for all concerned will likely prove a significant management challenge.

Health considerations aside, remote work arrangements appear to be paying off in other respects. According to a survey of 800 employers surveyed by Mercer— an international human resources and workplace benefits consulting firm—94 percent said that productivity was the same as or higher than it was before the pandemic, even with their employees working remotely.[12]

But, as with so many other aspects of 4IR, there's more than one side to this seeming predestination of remote work. According to a 2021 survey by the Netherlands-based research firm KPMG, a number of major employers no longer plan to cut back on office space to accommodate a greater percentage of remote employees. Many expect the majority of employees to return to their cubicles and on-site offices post-pandemic, with fewer than one-third of CEOs planning for a significant number of employees working elsewhere up to three days per week.[13]

Still, technology has and will continue to drive workplace change. Rather than an "all-or-nothing" approach—either full-time remote or on-site—many expect employers to consider something of a hybrid model that incorporates both work options. While allowing workers to continue to enjoy many of the benefits of remote work—such as a greater work-life balance and overall flexibility—a blended system would also include regular time spent in the office. That, say many executives, will serve to bolster company culture, something that they're concerned may be compromised by an exclusively remote arrangement.

THE TRANSACTIONAL BOSS VERSUS THE TRANSFORMATIONAL BOSS

Transactional leadership narrative:

Boss: Jim, now that COVID-19 is winding down, I'd like to speak to you about something.

Employee: Sure. What's up?

Boss: Well, as you know, ours is a company with a long, successful history.

Employee: I do, and I'm thankful for the opportunity.

continued

Boss: Well, to continue that history of success, I think it's critical that we get back to normal as soon as possible.

Employee: I couldn't agree more.

Boss: Well, that leads me to the topic at hand. I know you've been working remotely for a number of months now, and I want you to plan on returning to on-site work as quickly as possible.

Employee: Well, sir, I hope you're open to discussing this. I've really enjoyed my time working from home. It's been wonderful seeing my kids as much as I have, not to mention avoiding an hour's commute on the train.

Boss: I get all that. I'm glad you've enjoyed it. But, as I said, we need to get back to normal.

Employee: My work hasn't suffered, has it?

Boss: Not at all. In fact, your performance has been terrific.

Employee: So, what's the issue?

Boss: It's just that this is the way we've always done things. Look, I promise you I'll make it worth your while the next time salary reviews come up. Team players get rewarded, you know.

Employee: But it's not the money, sir. I like working from home. And it's worked out for everyone.

Boss (shaking his head, walking away): Jim, I hope you know what an awkward position this puts me in.

Transformational leadership narrative:

Boss: Jim, now that COVID-19 is winding down, I'd like to speak to you about something.

Employee: Sure. What's up?

Boss: Well, as you know, ours is a company with a long, successful history.

Employee: I do, and I'm thankful for the opportunity.

Boss: Well, to continue that history of success, I think it's critical that we get back to normal as soon as possible.

Employee: I couldn't agree more.

Boss: Well, that leads me to the topic at hand. I know you've been working remotely for a number of months now. Your performance has been terrific.

Employee: Thanks. I've really enjoyed it, seeing my kids more, not to mention avoiding that freeway commute.

Boss: I really appreciate that. But, traditionally, we've been a company where everyone works on-site. We feel it builds a sense of teamwork.

Employee: You want me to come back here full time?

Boss: Well, it's the way we've always done things . . .

Employee: Well, could we compromise some? Say, two days in the office, and three days from home? That way, I can be here when it's essential for me to be here and still have some time working from home.

Boss: I think that's an idea that warrants serious consideration. Could you draw up the specifics for me? Off the top of my head, I don't know why that wouldn't work just fine.

—Jeff Wuorio and Shelley Moench-Kelly

Some research has suggested that strength of culture may not necessarily depend quite so much on worker logistics. Rather, a clear definition of a company or organization's values that incorporate the benefits of remote work can serve to actually strengthen group culture—a leadership challenge moving forward as remote work arrangements of all sorts become more commonplace.

Related to more widespread remote work is a greater emphasis on work-life balance, as those working away from an office setting embrace benefits ranging from a greater sense of independence and autonomy to more time with friends and loved ones. However, this has also proven to be something of a double-edged sword. While many workers enjoy the flexibility and freedom of working from home, loneliness and isolation can also occur, as well as a blurring of work-life separation. That will make mental health another leadership priority.

A greater openness and access to the tools necessary to make remote work effective have also contributed to the increased appeal of freelancing over more conventional full-time employment. Not only did freelancers contribute some \$1.28 trillion to the US pre-pandemic economy in 2018, but projections also hold that the "gig economy" will make up 50 percent of the entire domestic workforce by 2027—the fastest-growing segment of the working population.[14] Remote platforms that allow freelancers to sell their work, such as Upwork, Freelancer, and TaskRabbit, will boost this growth.

Although growing use of freelancers will afford workers greater flexibility and opportunity to specifically craft their professional lives, companies and organizations looking for the stability of long employee tenures will have to adapt themselves as well to foster a similar level of loyalty and sense of connection among freelancers—a new challenge that will mandate different leadership, thinking, and action.

LOYALTY AND CONNECTION

As a writer, I have worked as a freelancer for most of my professional life. The advantages are almost too many to count—the flexibility, the freedom to choose those projects that interested me the most, not to mention the fact that I truly had the chance to watch my kids grow up. That's something that many of my friends in more "traditional" forms of work really missed out on, unfortunately.

As the workplace universe shifts toward greater use of freelancers and other forms of employee flexibility, it's understandable that many employers are anxious about trying to foster loyalty and a sense of common mission among workers who are technically *not* employees. In my experience, that concern may be overblown. When I've worked for individuals and companies in a freelance fashion, the fact that I was not an "employee" never stood in the way of my enthusiasm and loyalty—provided that I was treated with respect and dignity. To me, the message is clear—if an employer is empathetic,

> supportive, and honest, they'll inevitably attract and retain talented
> people, no matter if they're an on-site, a "nine-to-fiver," or a free-
> lancer living thousands of miles away. When it comes to loyalty and
> a sense of connection, labels really don't matter.
>
> —Jeff Wuorio

But, true to its extraordinarily pervasive nature, 4IR's impact has gone—and will continue to go—well beyond the purview of business and work. One such area is medicine, where the use of AI is already being explored in depth.

One general point of focus is the use of technology in more predictive health-care operational models. Given the enormous amount of existing data related to medicine, technology is increasingly used in proactive health care, as opposed to simply treating illness when it occurs. Moreover, AI has been shown to be more effective than human physicians in diagnosing a variety of diseases and conditions. To that end, pharmaceutical company Bayer has recently been working with tech companies to create software to help diagnose complex and unusual conditions, as well as help develop new drugs to treat these diseases.[15]

The very focus of medicine will also shift. The future of health care will be centered on the patient as consumer. Round-the-clock access to data and information—including data regarding cost of care—will place consumers at the very heart of their health and well-being. Devices such as wearable health trackers—largely unheard of only a few years ago—are just one signal of this consumer focus. Further, evolving technology will shift the logistics of care. In addition to care afforded by growing use of telehealth, sophisticated tests and tools could also mean more diagnoses (and care) taking place at home. That will free up space and resources at on-site care facilities for more involved and sophisticated treatment and procedures.

MY COVID BREAK

I am an artist, and I've made my living for nearly 50 years by promoting my artwork in galleries, coffee shops, and cafés. When COVID-19 hit, there was so much confusion as to how it was transmitted, where it originated, and how contagious it was. It reminded me of the AIDS crisis 40 years ago, only now, you could get COVID-19 from the little old lady next door or from someone in a crowd of people who was asymptomatic. Because I don't have health insurance, I immediately isolated myself. My business suffered because I wasn't physically interacting with my clients or the places I displayed my work, and I quickly blew through my meager savings account. Then a friend introduced me to Zoom as a way of keeping my work relevant, as well as marketing it to new buyers. He helped me set up my first meeting, which included my contacts from those galleries, coffee shops, and cafés, as well as their friends and colleagues. Not only were they able to drum up clients and customers for their own virtual showings and burgeoning take-out and carry-out services that erupted all over the city, but they also served as word-of-mouth advertising for me. I started a website and kept having the Zoom meetings with growing numbers of potential clients, and within three months I was able to support myself once again. It's a weird blessing in disguise, this pandemic. I never imagined I'd be selling my work via the internet. I always thought it had to be an in-person experience and that doing anything else would be a sell-out, that I wouldn't be true to my art. I experienced a roller coaster of emotions, and I know the world is still entrenched in the pandemic's effects, but the adage of "lead, follow, or get out of the way" really resonated with me and helped me develop an open mind to things I was previously afraid of.

—F. L., Artist, New York City, NY

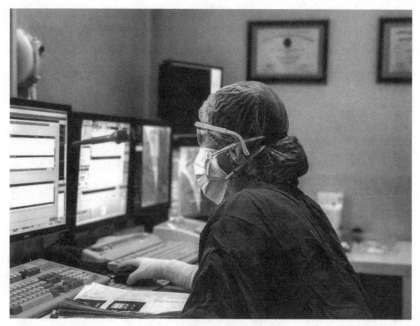

Fig. 1.2. Photo by Irwan Iwe on Unsplash.

Shifts in the working and professional environment will also bring about a significant change in education. Given that many mainstream jobs are being minimized or eliminated completely by technology, education in the next decade will become experiential and more focused on students gaining employable skills while still in school. With continued growth in remote learning, students will have greater options and control over where—and how—they learn. In turn, leaders will be compelled to think and act differently to adjust to this newfound empowerment.

With regard to education, perhaps the most visible impact of 4IR has been the growth of technology-based delivery systems, such as Zoom classes, online learning platforms, and other methods made particularly necessary during the COVID-19 pandemic. But equally significant is technology's impact on the content of education itself. Substantial changes to science and technology curricula will be necessary for students to acquire skills in the rapidly emerging areas of genomics, data science, AI, robotics, and nanomaterials, to cite just a few areas.

Specific examples of reframed science curriculum include several innovations at California-based Stanford University, where a new course, Problem Solving in Biology, allows students to design experiments to develop cures to real-world pathogens such as Lyme disease and HIV/AIDS. Additionally, a new course in engineering biology allows students to design their own computer-based life-forms on computers to solve practical problems in medicine, public health, and environmental management.[16]

The Fourth Industrial Revolution is also reshaping consumer habits. Taking the issue of remote one step further is the rise of the "homebody" economy. From fashion to food and entertainment to health care, consumers are increasingly focused on goods and services geared to home use.

Health care offers an ideal example—telehealth services. A field that struggled to gain consumer acceptance only a few years ago is now exploding, as patients come to experience and trust medical care performed over the internet. Although the telehealth field displays few signs of a pullback once the pandemic is under control, it does highlight the challenge of racial issues, as some minority groups may lack the level of internet access that others take for granted—another problematic issue that will need to be addressed.

The one-two punch of 4IR and the COVID-19 pandemic has also revolutionized the very structure of consumer activity. Sheer convenience coupled with lingering concern about virus transmission has led to the rise of contactless purchasing in stores and using QR codes or apps such as Apple Pay and Google Pay. Cards now use near-field communication for fast, convenient transactions without the need for any sort of physical contact. Digital wallets are gaining in popularity. China-based technology giant Alibaba has even developed a Smile-to-Pay functionality that incorporates facial recognition.[17]

THE FOURTH INDUSTRIAL REVOLUTION

Greater connection to information and resources has also resulted in a significant drop in traditional consumer loyalties. Recent research has found that 75 percent of American consumers are trying a new shopping behavior in response to economic pressures, store closings, and changing priorities.[18] This general change in behavior has also been reflected in a weakening of brand loyalty, with 36 percent of consumers trying a new product brand and 25 percent incorporating a new private-label brand. Businesses of all types will be compelled to rise to the challenge of connecting with consumers and building loyalty amid an environment that is effectively hindering them.

More specifically, AI will play a pivotal role in e-commerce in the future, in every sector of the industry from user experience to marketing to fulfillment and distribution. It seems clear that AI will continue to drive e-commerce, including through the use of chatbots, shopper personalization, image-based targeted advertising, and warehouse and inventory automation.

Not surprisingly, however, the advent of the Fourth Industrial Revolution also carries a variety of genuine risks. One global concern has to do with regulation. Given that market acceptance has only occurred over the past several years, AI is now only lightly regulated. As a result, the AI research community and government policy makers have recently argued for the need to strengthen the governance of AI.

In a 2015 article, "Benefits and Risks of Artificial Intelligence," Tom Ditteriech of Oregon State University cites three overriding risks:

- **Software quality.** Given the increasing complexity of AI systems and their use in critical roles such as controlling automobiles, surgical robots, and weapons systems, software reliability is of paramount concern.

- **Cyberattacks.** AI algorithms are no different from other software in terms of their vulnerability to cyberattack. But because AI algorithms are often charged with making high-stakes decisions—such as driving cars and directing robots—the impact of successful cyberattacks on AI systems could be much more devastating than attacks in the past that often focused on obtaining confidential, personal information.

- **Appropriate response.** An important aspect of any AI system that interacts with people is that it must "reason" about what people genuinely intend rather than carrying out commands in a literal, more rote manner. An AI system should not only act on a set of rules that it is instructed to obey—it must also analyze and understand whether the behavior that a human is requesting is likely to be judged as "normal" or "reasonable" by most people. It should also be continuously monitoring itself to detect abnormal internal behaviors, which might signal bugs, cyberattacks, or failures in its understanding of its actions.[19]

Security concerns can also be highly personal, even among those who otherwise welcome more widespread use of all sorts of technology. In a 2019 consumer survey, the online publication *Digital Pulse* reported 70 percent of respondents said Fourth Industrial Revolution technologies made their lives easier. At the same time, however, 68 percent expressed concern about the collection of their data, as well as potential assaults on their privacy and security, particularly with regard to technologies that track their locations.[20]

Another area of concern is the quality of relevant data. Information can itself carry bias and reflect societal inequities or the implicit biases of the designers who create and input the data. If there is bias in the data that is introduced into an AI tool, this bias is likely to carry over to the results generated by AI. To that end, there has even been a bill introduced into Congress titled the Algorithmic Accountability Act with the goal of forcing the Federal Trade Commission to investigate the use of any new AI technology for the potential to perpetuate bias.

The varied, possible impact of AI also carries significant political and inequality ramifications. In an op-ed piece in *The New York Times* in early 2021, columnist Thomas Edsall cited MIT economist Daron Acemoglu: "A.I. is in its infancy. It can be used for many things, some of them very complementary to humans. But right now it is going more and more in the direction of displacing humans, like a classic automation technology. Put differently, the current business model of leading tech companies is pushing A.I. in a predominantly automation direction."[21]

That, Acemoglu added, will likely have a negative impact on less educated populations while benefitting those with higher levels of education—for instance, displacing factory workers as professions with higher skill levels such as engineering and finance grow in demand. In turn, says Harvard economist Dani Rodrick, that could exacerbate the growing divide between so-called red and blue states: "Automation hits the electorate the same way that deindustrialization and globalization have done, hollowing out the middle classes and enlarging the potential vote base of right-wing populists—especially if corrective policies are not in place."[22]

Still, from a global perspective, the advent of the Fourth Industrial Revolution has propelled the individual to a particularly visible and influential position, be it in business, health care, education, or other areas. This development has produced a greater focus on the end user rather than a more hierarchical, top-heavy form of authority and direction. Increasingly, the individual is in the driver's seat and seems unlikely to relinquish it in the immediate future.

Interestingly, however, the growing focus on the individual has not created an "every person for him- or herself" mentality. Rather, there's an ever-growing sense of collective empowerment. This collective mentality, which was also fostered by the challenges of the COVID-19 pandemic, has motivated a community-focused consumer mindset—even in traditionally individualistic cultures—that has put mutual support and advocacy at the forefront of various forms of behavior, be they political or consumer related. That, in turn, should motivate the public sector, business, and other areas to prioritize user empowerment to boost anything from citizen involvement and satisfaction to customer retention. How leaders think and react will be critical to such an effective response.

CHAPTER 1 LEARN AND TRANSFORM

1. The Fourth Industrial Revolution and other drivers of change have shifted the playing field as far as work is concerned. Although the COVID-19 pandemic was an absolute tragedy in most ways, it did compel people to acknowledge that the Fourth Industrial Revolution has opened up work arrangements and tools that previously received little attention. Moving forward, a number of noteworthy companies and organizations have publicly committed to continue to offer a variety of work options, including full-time remote employment. Those companies that emulate that policy—at least to the point of making part-time remote work available—will be well positioned to recruit and retain top-tier talent. The argument that "this is the way we've always done things" will hold little sway for employees who recognize that some companies are more forward-thinking than others—and they'll vote with their feet by going somewhere else to work.

2. One downside to the proliferation of the Fourth Industrial Revolution is a sharpened, justifiable concern over security and privacy, be it proprietary work material or medical records. As technology continues to spread and mature, it will be incumbent upon

companies and organizations of all types to invest in and maintain rigorous security measures and protocols. Just as important, they also need to inform employees, customers, and others of all that they're doing to ensure that sensitive information and data remain secure. Lacking that sense of trust, many will be understandably gun-shy about using even the most advantageous and sophisticated technology—particularly so in an age where misinformation can cloud and distort well-intentioned and well-executed policies.

3. It's clear that the new technology that characterizes 4IR can optimize the way people work—provided it is implemented thoughtfully. However tempting it can be just to load up on every new form of tech that comes down the road, it's critical to support that commitment with systemic planning. That means identifying viable time frames to introduce new tools and comprehensive training for employees and others using that technology. Not only can thoughtful planning and subsequent execution produce better, longer-lasting results, but also those who learn and become adept at using technology will better understand that such tools will be used to augment and support—not replace—a living, breathing workforce.

CHAPTER 2

COVID-19

IN MID-2020, only a few months before succumbing to cancer, Rabbi Jonathan Sacks of Great Britain observed that COVID-19 was probably the closest an atheist might come to a revelation.[1]

Rabbi Sacks—a member of the House of Lords—was spot-on with his comment. In many ways, the COVID-19 pandemic served as a worldwide punch in the stomach. If nothing else, it was shocking to many that such a catastrophe could occur, not to mention the checkerboard of spotty global response that only served to strengthen its path of destruction.

He was equally on point with another remark—that the pandemic brought out the worst in all of us, as well as the best. In many ways, COVID-19 has, in fact, served to highlight our best selves in addition to far less appealing aspects.

That goes for society as a whole, not just how individuals behaved and reacted during the crisis. In many ways, it's underscored many of society's greatest attributes along with a number of glaring flaws.

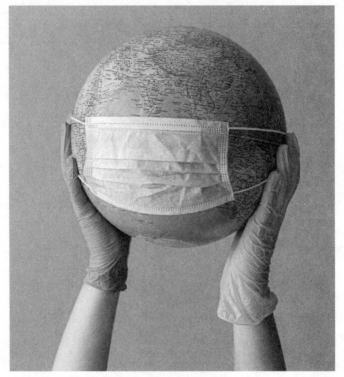

Fig. 2.1. Photo by Anna Shvets from Pexels.

It's become a cliché to say that the world is not going back to the way things were pre-COVID-19. Looked at in another way, it really has no choice—for better or worse, the pandemic has served to refocus our attention in any number of directions. Moving forward, it's going to be that much harder to keep looking away, particularly from things that we may prefer not to see.

The prior chapter touched on the role of the Fourth Industrial Revolution (4IR) as a powerful catalyst in upending work, careers, and various aspects of our professional lives. If 4IR helped kickstart the work-from-home movement in a meaningful way, the COVID-19 pandemic served to accelerate its spread and acceptance—or, at the very least, the possibility that work no longer need be confined to an office building.

The statistics are eye-opening. Before the COVID-19 outbreak, only 7 percent of workers in the United States had access to a "flexible workplace" benefit—or telework—according to a report by the Pew Research Center.[2] In contrast, a 2020 Gartner survey of 229 human resources departments showed that roughly one-half of participating companies had more than 80 percent of their employees working from home during the early stages of the pandemic. Further, 47 percent said they intended to allow employees to work from a remote location full time post-COVID-19.[3]

That's encouraging news for many, particularly for those who, perhaps to their own surprise, flourished in a remote work arrangement. But despite the varied benefits of increased work options—from greater productivity to boosts in employee satisfaction—that shift also highlighted a discouraging underbelly. As the Pew report points out, prior to COVID-19, flexible work arrangements were largely the purview of a fortunate few. Although many jobs by their nature prohibit anything but on-site work, working from home, telecommuting, and other such options were largely available to persons in higher-paying positions—so-called knowledge workers such as lawyers, scientists, engineers, and persons in high-level management roles. As Pew notes, the higher the pay scale, the greater the access to a variety of work arrangements.

HEALTH FOR EVERYONE

My company is a large car rental conglomerate, and I'm a project manager. The atmosphere has always been one of old-school "do this or don't come back on Monday" practice, and most of the employees worked in fear of losing their jobs because of minor missteps that might enrage upper management . . . management far above my pay grade. When the pandemic hit, it hit Southern California as hard as it did New York. Our society is very outdoorsy and social, and so many people ignored the warnings for so long. I'm amazed that my

continued

company was one of the earliest to adopt a work-from-home option with no questions asked. But the employees were almost like caged veal. They couldn't process this decision. It was as if they'd just been freed of their cages into a green pasture and didn't know what to do. None of them trusted upper management. When upper management realized no one was taking them up on the work-from-home option, they held departmental meetings to encourage the employees to take it not only for their own health and that of their families but also for the health of the company. It took a pandemic for them to emerge from their ivory towers and interact with the human beings that made them rich. COVID-19 leveled us all, from the youngest clerk to the company founder. Who knows if the powers that be enacted the work-from-home option out of true caring for their employees or as a self-serving shield against potential lawsuits? I'd like to think it was out of caring. I don't think any of them are evil; I just think they got stuck in the seemingly enviable positions of wielding power and status over others. In the end (or what I hope is the end), 90 percent of the employees elected to stay at home, and the company has supported them. It has sold many of its physical buildings and leased satellite offices for those who opt to work in them from time to time. I never thought I'd see a working format like this, but I'm glad it exists.

—J. S., Project Manager, Glendale, CA

In other words, the COVID-19-driven pivot to different work structures uncovered a pervasive form of workplace inequality. While highly paid employees could access the advantages of working where—and in some cases, *when*—they wished, those in lesser-paying jobs enjoyed no such flexibility. As the Pew report summarizes, "In that respect, COVID-19 may yet do what years of advocacy have failed to: Make telework a benefit available to more than a relative handful of US workers."

For those who can work from home for the first time, the new policies offer an escape from endless commutes and lost time with family and friends. They also allow workers to move to other potentially less expensive or more attractive locations, farther from city centers or office complexes—not to mention relocating to more desirable areas of the country or even overseas.

LESSONS FOR LIVING

We're now living and operating in a very different world than the one that existed just a couple of years ago. No one really knows what's coming around the next corner; we're all operating on uneven footing. Still, leaders' jobs haven't fundamentally changed—we still need to spark creativity, drive progress, and ensure sustainability.

So I've been reminding myself that while I can't predict the future, I can at least try to prepare to live in it, make sense of it, and navigate whatever upheavals arise as strategically as possible.

And to do that, I keep going back to these tried-and-true lessons:[4]

1. Accept Your Battle

As humans, our instincts are to fight bitterly against adversity. The most resilient among us will often find a way to fight it by embracing it.

On my desk, I have a copy of *The Last Lecture* by Randy Pausch.[5] Very few have talked about embracing adversity like him. He was a professor at Carnegie Mellon and a husband and father of three. He was diagnosed with pancreatic cancer and given only a few months to live. He gave his last lecture on September 18, 2007. His story, and in particular this final lecture, are a powerful reminder of the strength of the human spirit.

"Another way to be prepared is to think negatively," Randy said. "Yes, I'm a great optimist. But, when trying to make a decision, I often think of the worst-case scenario. I call it 'the eaten by wolves factor.' If I do something, what's the most terrible thing that could happen? Would I be eaten by wolves? One thing that makes it possible to be an optimist, is if you have a contingency plan for when all hell breaks loose. There are a lot of things I don't worry about, because I have a plan in place if they do."

continued

Randy decided to accept his situation and live out the days he had remaining by making a difference. He died on July 25, 2008, and now he lives on not only through his family but also through the millions he inspired. I am certainly one of them. If you haven't read *The Last Lecture* or seen its video, then you must. Once we accept our situation, it allows us to adapt and even thrive in the face of adversity.

2. Leverage Your Solitude

From Beethoven to Newton to Buddha to Darwin, all experienced critical awakenings during self-imposed solitary periods. The psychologist and author Rollo May explained this phenomenon very well in his book *The Courage to Create*. "In order to be open to creativity," he wrote, "one must have the capacity for constructive use of solitude. One must overcome the fear of being alone."[6]

Nicola Tesla, one of the greatest innovators of all time, concurred: "The mind is sharper and keener in seclusion and uninterrupted solitude. Originality thrives in seclusion free of outside influences beating upon us to cripple the creative mind. Be alone—that is the secret of invention: Be alone, that is when ideas are born."[7]

These days, we now have the evidence to support those claims. Research conducted by Greg Feist of San Jose State University found that when people let their focus shift away from others around them, they're better able to engage in "metacognition," the process of thinking critically and reflectively about your own thoughts.[8]

Sometimes we need to slow down in order to move forward. Slowing down is a deliberate choice that can lead to greater appreciation for the inner and outer world. Being truly in the moment allows us to escape from adversity and conserve our inner energy. Solitude allows us to slow down.

3. Guide Your Energy

In many ways, our thoughts control our lives. Negative thinking attracts negative energy; positive thinking attracts positive energy. Buddha, Aristotle, and many others have suggested the same: how we think creates the energy that ultimately manifests our realities. If we go into a situation with a negative thought process, then we are almost destined to have a negative outcome.

This also applies to group thinking or collective consciousness. When a collection of people together guides their mental energy for a positive outcome, the likelihood of their success is usually a lot higher. Their collective energy attracts positivity or negativity.

Lao Tzu said, "Water is fluid, soft, and yielding. But water will wear away rock, which is rigid and cannot yield. As a rule, whatever is fluid, soft, and yielding will overcome whatever is rigid and hard. This is another paradox: What is soft is strong."[9]

Our ability to effectively survive, thrive, and lead comes from flexibly riding out our ups and downs. Life's journey does not always come from blasting through rocks and impediments, but rather from having the faith, resilience, and adaptability to cope with the harsh realities of life.

The physical reaction to fear and pain is called the "fight-or-flight" response. Being mindful is the exact opposite of that response. Mindful living comes from "letting go." Letting go is the inner action that stops resisting fear and pain. It allows us to restore our ability to see clearly.

The people we surround ourselves with (virtually or physically) greatly impact our daily energy. Spending time with people who make you stronger requires intentional effort and is a key component in being able to move forward. Equally important is to avoid people who bring us down, waste our time, take us backward, and have no interest in our suffering.

4. Achieve Small Goals Every Day

I set priorities for the beginning of the day the night before. These priorities are not only based on the importance of the goals but also based on the prospect of completion.

If we want to be productive with our time and manage it well, we need to spend our time working toward achieving smaller goals with a series of small tasks. Setting smaller goals for ourselves offers us positive reinforcement when we achieve them. It feels good to know that I am accomplishing something. It helps keep me motivated and encouraged at working toward my bigger goals and aspirations.

As retired US Navy admiral William Harry McRaven so famously said, "If you want to change the world, start off by making your

continued

bed . . . If you make your bed every morning you will have accomplished the first task of the day. It will give you a small sense of pride, and it will encourage you to do another task and another and another. And by the end of the day, that one task completed, will have turned into many tasks completed."[10]

There is a saying that 80 percent of our accomplishments come from 20 percent of our efforts. So what 20 percent of our work is the most valuable? Once we've identified it, focusing the lion's share of our time and energy in that direction creates progress. Selecting the right success indicators to drive our activities creates the tasks we can knock out first for the greatest impact.

5. Influence Others, Then Let Them Influence You

Managing crisis means accepting incredible levels of uncertainty with a calm, cool, and positive attitude. That's never easy. But the sense of urgency to tackle tough situations always requires an even temper. In order to communicate a decisive yet flexible plan as soon as crisis hits, you'll need to assess the situation effectively:

- Ask yourself: What does this situation demand? Is it a personal crisis, a systemic crisis, or a contextual one?
- Then craft an immediate-term response strategy based on how you want to emerge from this crisis at the end—even if you don't know exactly how you'll get there—and communicate it to your team, partners, and customers.
- Finally, as you begin rolling out that strategy, keep an eye on ability (your own and your organization's) to communicate and execute it based on how the crisis evolves (and it will!)—without losing sight of your assets, structure, and capabilities.

True leaders inspire and influence everyone in good times and bad—their executive team, employees, customers, clients, partners, and many others. Even if some decisions involve the most basic of gut instincts, leaders navigating crises need to tell their teams precisely what they want, when, and why—then help them make it happen. Waiting too long to weigh countervailing opinions can spell doom.

Communicating effectively in times of uncertainty means not just articulating your point of view but also listening actively—without bias or judgment and with a real willingness to consider different per-spectives. That means paying heed not just to the content of others' ideas but to their emotional tone, too. Both are crucial for mutual understanding—and, ultimately, everyone getting back on their feet.

6. Empathy Always Pays Dividends

For communication to get through on all sides, we have to be clear about what we want from each other. That's true all the time, but especially so during periods of high uncertainty.

There's no way to start working toward a common goal until everyone understands what it is and what's expected of them to help achieve it. As a leader, I try especially hard to remain approach-able and keep an open dialogue flowing. It's harder to keep everyone motivated, asking questions, and sharing their concerns when a lot is changing. But getting it right just means doubling down on the type of empathy leaders love to talk about under much steadier conditions.

This means not just clearly articulating our message but also listening actively—without bias or judgment and with a real willing-ness to consider different perspectives. Again, this is an adage so familiar that it almost sounds trite, but it's something I keep coming back to these days. It's about trading messages respectfully and accurately, not just delivering them. Paying heed to their factual and emotional content makes for mutual understanding when that's badly needed.

Leaders may feel their job is to reassure their teams—to talk more than they're used to. But I've found listening to be even more important. When I'm actively listening, I'll hear genuine concerns and clear a space for talking levelheadedly about how to cope with them together.

7. No Matter What, Move Forward

Humans are resilient creatures. We have a natural capacity to move toward the light, to make the most of bad situations. In turmoil, I know that it's paramount for me to define a better vision for the future. But there's a risk of getting too philosophical and losing your momentum, your impulse toward action.

I've found that in trying to instill a sense of mission and purpose in my organization, I need to keep underscoring the urgency of the tasks at hand. No mission is static. It's never just a matter of principles. It's what you do about them that counts. Purpose-driven organizations act and adapt. No matter the political, social, or economic climate, there's always a way to find new market spaces or gaps in existing ones. There are always problems to solve.

To stay agile and respond to changes my team and I can never predict, I try to keep asking myself the following questions:

- What product or service needs, technologies, and socio-economic factors are already changing—no matter what we might be doing about them?

- What are my most socioeconomically impactful strategies? Where will they be in the next quarter or the next year?

- What does my organization do well right now? What have we always done better than anybody?

- What can we do better by finding new partners or collaborators or by considering mergers and acquisitions?

This is a useful checklist all the time, of course, but I try to keep it front and center during periods of rapid change. If change is embedded in everything you do already, then adapting to a period of turmoil won't seem like such a foreign concept. In my experience, that takes a culture of experimentation and responsibility. When things are going well, innovation tends to offer incremental benefits, but when circumstances demand making big shifts quickly, you need everyone to know it's incumbent on them to take risks and that they have the liberty to do so.

You may not know what's coming next, but the thing about uncertainty is that it's never an unfamiliar feeling. There was an earlier moment where you felt just as uncertain, but you somehow made it through. For me, anyway, the key isn't just to wait it out; it's also what you do—together—that makes all the difference.

—Faisal Hoque

Again, however, the work-at-home catalyst supplied by COVID-19 carries caveats. While many workers enjoy the flexibility and freedom of working from home, loneliness and isolation can mar the experience, and work-life separation can also become blurred (without having to physically leave the workplace, it can become difficult to recognize when the workday begins and ends). That will make mental health and workplace culture that emphasizes overall balance a leadership priority. Additionally, many leaders accustomed to close monitoring of employee performance will be challenged to accept and work within greater employee autonomy and independence (it's easy to picture chronic micromanagers yanking out their hair by the bale in frustration). These and other issues will require new thinking and action to fully leverage the possibilities of remote workers while addressing the potential downsides.

ALONE, NOT ISOLATED

I have worked from a home office for most of my adult life. From a work standpoint, the COVID-19 pandemic did little to upend my work routine and logistics, save for a greater number of meetings via Zoom and other like technology. However, I can attest to concerns surrounding isolation and loneliness. Although I feel my productivity has always benefited from a somewhat isolated work setting, the lack of meaningful interaction with others—even to the point of a casual conversation during a break—did on occasion feel particularly insulated, especially during the early stages of the pandemic when lockdowns were both pervasive and strict. Fortunately, thanks to the experiential learning experience of a long-standing, solitary work environment, I went to particular lengths to maintain ongoing contact with family and friends as much as possible. Phone calls, emails, social media, and other means helped me feel separated but not necessarily isolated. Anyone considering the possibility of working remotely should honestly consider the

continued

impact of occasional bouts of isolation and, from there, consider proactively what they can do to enjoy the advantages of remote work without feeling needlessly apart from others. That may mean a hybrid schedule of remote and on-site employment or returning to in-person work full time. Not every work arrangement is flawless, and COVID-19 helped show us that remote work does have its pitfalls, as well as its pluses.

—Jeff Wuorio

There are other problematic consequences. Any remote work arrangement is far from perfect, whether that manifests in feelings of isolation or the understandable challenges of remote workers with young children at home. Additionally, younger workers will also be challenged to develop beneficial mentor relationships, a valuable dynamic nearly impossible to cultivate when contact is limited to Zoom meetings and telephone calls. Accordingly, some employment experts are urging younger employees to return to an in-house office setting as quickly as possible—if even merely on a part-time basis—so as not to lose out on the value and insight that a relationship with a mentor can provide.

Looked at from a broader perspective, the COVID-19 pandemic has also highlighted long-standing global economic issues. The troubling disparity in infection rates and their consequences clearly reflect significant economic inequality. Developing economies were hit early and hard by the pandemic, showcasing a continued lack of global support and cooperation among more established nations.

In response to that and other challenges, many experts are calling for proactive, global-wide planning—similar to the Bretton Woods Conference in Bretton Woods, New Hampshire, near the end of World War II that addressed postwar, worldwide monetary issues. But while Bretton Woods took place amid an environment of widespread unity against a common foe, cooperation between nations will likely be much more difficult to achieve today. From the so-called America First movement to France's National Rally and Austria's Freedom Party, there's a growing worldwide drumbeat of "my country first" that threatens to undercut any sort of meaningful cooperation. Governments, politicians, thought leaders, and others hoping for a greater sense of common cause will clearly be challenged to overcome those varied hurdles and establish some sort of far-reaching social and economic contract.

But the economic revelations aren't exclusively discouraging. For instance, a number of economies—Poland and France among them—adopted versions of Germany's highly effective *Kurzarbeit* (short work) subsidy during the pandemic. While the policy means fewer hours and lower pay for workers, government compensation payments partially offset the shortfall. By keeping workers on the job—albeit with less financial reward—economic recovery is positioned to fall into place that much faster, so much so that some economists have labeled the program one of Germany's most attractive and successful exports.[11]

As with the Fourth Industrial Revolution, COVID-19's disruption has been consistently democratic—few areas of our lives have been spared some level of impact. With regard to education, one writer has labeled COVID-19 America's "Sputnik Moment," referring to the Soviet Union's 1957 satellite launch that, in turn, pushed American education to a much greater emphasis on science and mathematics. So, too, has the pandemic prompted concern over the return to "normal" education—a system deemed by many to be broken in any number of ways.[12]

Coupled with fast-spreading, rapidly maturing technology, the pandemic has helped further cement the role of remote learning. The dynamics of education may also shift in other ways. While distance learning will continue to be primarily teacher designed and led, the growth of remote learning will also afford students greater freedom and increased options as to how they pursue their educations. As a result, teachers could evolve to be more of a reference point or touchstone in the learning process as opposed to a traditional "instructor."

COVID-19 has also propelled significant change—with certainly more to come—in higher education. Perhaps first and foremost on students', families', and employees' minds is when colleges and universities will be able to return to any sort of environment that even approximates pre-pandemic conditions. As of this writing, institutions are considering a variety of options, including mandated vaccinations, continued limits on the size of gatherings from classes to commencements, and other issues central to a safe resumption of activities.

More specifically, many schools, such as the University of California and the University of Maryland, have announced that COVID-19 vaccinations will be mandatory for all students and employees. A number of private schools, such as Harvard and Minnesota-based Carleton, are also requiring vaccinations. By contrast, several colleges in northeastern Iowa have said they don't plan to impose any such requirements (Florida recently passed a law specifically outlawing those sorts of prohibitions at state schools, prompting several schools to reverse what had been vaccination mandates). In yet another twist, some schools are dangling financial incentives to entice student vaccinations. At Rowan University in New Jersey, full-time students who provide proof of vaccination receive a $500 credit on course registration, and students who live on campus receive a $500 housing credit.[13]

Higher education is certainly motivated from a financial standpoint to do everything possible to return to normal activities as quickly and completely as possible. For one thing, failing to do so will almost certainly result in drops in revenue—in many cases, a significant falloff. There may be many closures, particularly among small private colleges with smaller endowments and tighter budget margins. State public systems may shut down and consolidate some campuses.

In yet another instance of empowered consumers, colleges and universities may also face backlash from students and families still seething from having to pay in-person prices for online learning during the pandemic. To date, lawyers have filed more than 300 cases on behalf of students and parents demanding refunds of tuition for educations they deemed substandard or not what they were told they would receive. Although legal experts have expressed doubt about the financial validity of such claims, noting the difficulty in proving education "malpractice," schools nonetheless will be challenged to establish—or reestablish—the genuine value of what they offer.

Accordingly, many colleges and universities, having been forced to migrate much of their curriculum online because of the pandemic, will likely maintain some form of online presence. While by no means a palatable substitute for in-person advocates, greater online offerings will certainly benefit those for whom a more traditional college experience simply isn't viable. Additionally, colleges and universities can leverage online programs to further showcase value, affordability, and access.

But whatever varied hybrids of in-person and remote instruction take hold at schools at all levels throughout the world, even the most effective adaptation can't obscure significant issues of inequality. First up is plunging student attendance. According to a survey by *Education Week*, average student absenteeism doubled during the pandemic, from an average of 5 percent pre-COVID-19 to 10 percent during the pandemic itself.[14]

A disproportionate number of those disengaged students are lower-income Black, Latino, and Indigenous children who have struggled to keep up in classrooms that are partly or fully remote. Underlying reasons include needing to support their families by working or caring for siblings, homelessness, poor English skills, and children whose parents work outside the home and struggle in the absence of adult supervision.

But poor internet service is another culprit—perhaps an even more ominous one. According to a study by Common Sense Media, approximately as many as 16 million K–12 public school students, or 30 percent of all public K–12 students, live in households either without an internet connection or without a device adequate for distance learning at home, a higher number than previously recorded. In Mississippi alone, approximately half of the state's students lack access to reliable broadband, the highest level of any state in the country.[15]

Despite the lack of comprehensive technology, the pandemic has helped usher in what seems likely to be a permanent network of distance learning options for K–12 students. Hundreds of the nation's 13,000 school districts have established virtual schools during the pandemic, with plans to continue to operate them for years to come, according to education researchers. Unlike COVID-19-driven programs pieced together out of sheer necessity, many virtual schools have their own teachers, who work exclusively with remote students and employ curricula geared specifically to online learning.

COVID-19 has also underscored the gross inadequacies of the American public health system. Not only did that system fail to quickly identify and control the spread of the coronavirus, but also the United States did not make testing widely available early in the pandemic and was late to impose physical distancing guidelines (due, in significant part, to destructive and tone-deaf political influence on public health issues). That, in turn, has raised the pressure on all levels of government, particularly the federal, to consider some type of reform to minimize the chance of a similarly disastrous response to future public health matters.

Continuing a discouraging theme, COVID-19 has further highlighted inequality in medical care across the globe. Even in countries with universal health care, such as Great Britain, individuals from Black and minority ethnic groups; poorer socioeconomic backgrounds; urban and rurally deprived locations; and other vulnerable groups of society were especially hard hit by inadequate health care.

The pandemic's impact has been particularly revealing regarding health-care conditions in the United States. Problems and hurdles regarding treatment of the disease and vaccination efforts notwithstanding, the pandemic has significantly undermined health insurance coverage in

America. A sudden surge in unemployment—exceeding 20 million workers—has caused many Americans to lose essential employer-sponsored insurance. Many will ultimately continue to go uninsured.

Sadly, whether insured or not, a growing segment of the population will also find convenient and effective access to health care more challenging. For the first time since the Great Depression, crippling financial losses threaten the viability of substantial numbers of hospitals and office practices. This is particularly true for those who were already financially vulnerable, including those in rural locations, safety-net providers, and primary care practices.

This all comes at a time when the value of proactive health is becoming increasingly evident. As COVID-19 has shown, it's imperative that systems and networks be put into place to better identify and respond to future public health crises. As some observers have pointed out, virus screening is likely to become part of everyday life, much as security measures became commonplace after the 9/11 terrorist attack. That, in turn, argues for significant investment in health-care infrastructure to proactively combat any future viral outbreaks and other widespread health issues.

MASKS—THE NEW NORMAL?

I was born and grew up near Tokyo, Japan, in the mid-1960s. Even back then, people wore masks as normal parts of their daily routines ... to protect themselves not only from pollution but also from others who might be sick and out in public. It is extremely rare for the Japanese worker (then and now) to call in sick unless he/she is suffering from a near-fatal illness or debilitating injury. The whole mindset of the Japanese culture is "we are not individuals, we are a nation" and that each person's contribution makes the nation strong, which goes way beyond national pride. The attitude is hardwired into each human being and is a living, breathing example of the oft-quoted stance of the *Star Trek* character Mr. Spock: "The needs of the many outweigh the needs of the few," to which Captain Kirk adds, "Or the

continued

one." It's pretty powerful and, in my experience, not often witnessed outside Japan. The only other time I've witnessed this mindset since my youth came during the COVID-19 pandemic and when I learned about New Zealand's immediate nationwide acceptance of mask wearing to stem the spread of the disease. There was an almost instantaneous realization and proactive action as a nation to band together and save its citizens from a deadly virus.

—Shelley Moench-Kelly

The pandemic's impact on consumer behavior parallels that of the Fourth Industrial Revolution in a number of ways. Coupling health concerns with convenience, COVID-19 has strengthened consumer flight to digital purchases. Food and household categories have seen an average of more than 30 percent growth in online customer base across countries.[16] Emphasizing both value and purchases deemed essential, consumers are also coming to question brand loyalty as innovative shopping options allow them to explore various products and services.

COVID-19 has been understandably devastating to travel and tourism—but just how destructive has surprised many industry observers and researchers. Unlike prior health crises that were far more limited to particular areas and sectors, the pandemic's effect on travel has been worldwide. As one research paper notes, recovery from the pandemic will almost certainly take longer than the "average" rebound time of 10 months and mandate significant public and private funding and support.[17] Concern about a sluggish recovery has prompted some destinations, ranging from Dracula's castle in Romania to Six Flags Great America Theme Park in Gurnee, Illinois, to announce plans to offer COVID-19 vaccinations to unvaccinated visitors.

But prohibitions and less overall movement also have had beneficial impacts on the environment. Coronavirus lockdowns, which bring the usual dynamics of metropolitan areas around the world to a near-grinding halt, have also appeared to dramatically reduce carbon dioxide emissions. A study published in mid-2020 in the journal *Nature Climate Change* found that daily global carbon dioxide emissions dropped by 17 percent in early 2020, compared with levels in 2019. In certain countries, that reduction was as high as 26 percent—overall, one of the biggest drops in recorded history.[18]

Unfortunately, those optimistic statistics are likely to be short-lived. Once post-pandemic global activity resumes, emissions are likely to rebound to prior levels. Moreover, as climate researchers have pointed out, one year or so of reduced emissions will barely make a dent in the overall level of carbon dioxide that has built up in the atmosphere for many years.

Fig. 2.2. Photo by Tim Mossholder from Pexels.

Given these and a variety of other aftereffects of the COVID-19 pandemic, government at all levels will be charged with responding to increasing demands for services, particularly as citizens' expectations for virtual and remote services have grown. Greater use of digital platforms and remote work could possibly reshape the makeup and the fundamental function of government. Adaptive and more fluid regulation are also viable possibilities.

In a nutshell, COVID-19 has served to open our eyes—not just to medical and public health matters but also to a number of societal issues that, given the hustle and bustle of "normal" life, were perhaps too easy to ignore. Whether we leverage that sharpened viewpoint to pursue meaningful change or work that much harder to continue to divert our attention remains to be seen.

Despite the devastation wrought by the pandemic, there's another crisis that has been festering much longer than COVID-19, so much so that, in the eyes of many, its ramifications and potential destruction will far outpace the damage that any virus could possibly cause.

CHAPTER 2 LEARN AND TRANSFORM

1. The impact of COVID-19 has highlighted the importance of one element of transformational leadership. Perhaps now more than ever, business leadership needs to emphasize empathy with clients and consumers. The pandemic has served to further consumers' growing emphasis on doing business with businesses that "do good," rather than just the least expensive choices. It's critical that businesses through various means—such as soliciting consumer feedback on a regular basis—stay in close touch with clients' values and priorities. Price is still an issue but no longer holds the singular dominance it once commanded. To succeed and grow, businesses and organizations of all types will need to empathize with their end users to make certain that their priorities are aligned with the person making a buying or some other sort of decision.

2. Empathy is a post-COVID-19 imperative, one that requires more careful thinking and execution than might be assumed.

At its core, being empathetic simply means prioritizing others' thoughts and feelings, but it's also important to establish strategies and systems with which to better understand others. For instance, in working to keep abreast of consumers' shifting values and priorities, companies and businesses need to consider carefully just how to connect with clients and customers. In addition to surveys and other means of acquiring feedback, tools such as blogs, newsletters, and other forms of outreach can be effective in proactively encouraging contact and discussion. Consider as well internal empathy strategies. Do employees and others within a company or organization feel valued and understood? Are there means available with which they can express their thoughts and experiences? Businesses and organizations that don't take actionable steps to build and promote an environment of empathy may find highly talented people looking elsewhere for more satisfying and enriching experiences. That's particularly so, given the propensity for disgruntled employees to air their grievances via social media.

3. As is the case with other areas, COVID-19 has placed students and their families firmly in the driver's seat when it comes to education. Rather than a more traditional hierarchical student-teacher relationship, students are enjoying a growing influence over what they learn and how they learn it, from remote learning options to more experiential forms of education. That will mandate genuine empathy on the part of teachers, administrators, and others in the education community. Listening and acting upon the input of students and their families will be critical to provide learning opportunities that are both meaningful and relevant. As with any empowered consumers, students and their families who feel they aren't being heard have many more options now to find an educational setting more in line with their desires and priorities.

CHAPTER 3

CLIMATE CHANGE

THE YEAR 2021 has certainly had more than its share of impactful events. From growing control over the devastating COVID-19 pandemic to exploding unrest in the Middle East, 2021 has handed the world a substantial list of things that warrant genuine concern.

However, neither a worldwide health crisis nor a region teetering on the brink of all-out war is as worrisome to the Switzerland-based World Economic Forum as an issue that has been festering for many years. In the group's 2021 *Global Risks Report*, extreme weather, climate action failure, and human environmental damage landed in the three top spots for significant risks by likelihood. For all the destruction wrought by COVID-19, infectious diseases finished out of the money at the fourth spot.[1]

How could climate-related issues muscle out a virus that has claimed the lives of millions? A heading in the group's risks report puts it both powerfully and succinctly: "No Vaccine for Environmental Degradation," adding that "failure to act would inevitably lead to catastrophic physical impacts and severe economic harm that would require costly policy responses."

The World Economic Forum is by no means a voice in the wilderness. In mid-2021, Switzerland-based Swiss Re Group, one of the world's largest providers of insurance to other insurance companies, released a report of its own warning that climate change threatened to cut the global economy by $23 trillion unless the world quickly slowed the use of fossil fuels. The report cited declining crop yields, rising seas and temperatures, and numerous other factors in its disturbing analysis.[2]

Fig. 3.1. Photo by Marcin Jozwiak from Pexels.

Nor are these sorts of warnings relatively new. A statement issued in Toronto in 1988 based on the views of scientists, policy makers, the United Nations, and international organizations warned that "humanity is conducting an unintended, uncontrolled, globally pervasive experiment whose ultimate consequences could be second only to nuclear war. The earth's atmosphere is being changed at an unprecedented rate by pollutants resulting from human activities, inefficient and wasteful fossil fuels, and the effects of rapid population growth in many regions. These changes are already having harmful consequences over many parts of the globe."[3]

Once more, vast inequality is at much of the heart of the problem and its consequences. The Swiss Re report suggests the fallout could be particularly damaging to Asian nations, including Malaysia, the Philippines, and Thailand, which could stand to lose as much as one-third of their overall wealth.

Additionally, potential economic harm to any country, regardless of its wealth and economic strength, carries global ramifications. As the world economy becomes increasingly interconnected and interdependent, climate issues in one country or region of the globe will likely impact economic conditions elsewhere.

Another reason climate change was cited as the top concern in the global risks report was, ironically enough, the COVID-19 pandemic that was listed as the fourth-greatest concern. Although widespread shutdowns have brought short-term drops in carbon emissions, the global struggle to bring the virus under control has understandably stretched countries' resources, not the least of which are financial. Less money to combat climate change—with funds being diverted to the pandemic—means governments are particularly ill-equipped to underwrite meaningful climate action.

Just as troubling, that issue may not be a short-term concern. Given how hard it is to forecast how varied governments and countries will recover economically, limited funds for climate change may persist into the future, prolonging and even exacerbating what many understandably see as a grossly inadequate response.

As it happens, the COVID-19 pandemic took place during a period when benchmarks of climate damage have only grown worse. Temperatures have continued to climb, and natural disasters are becoming unnervingly commonplace. The year 2019 was the second warmest on record for both land and ocean temperatures.[4] Lacking any impactful efforts to quickly implement policies and practices aimed at curbing climate change, that level of destruction only promises to grow at an increasingly exponential rate.

Few, if any, industries have been utterly immune to climate change's economic devastation. To that end, the decade from 2010 to 2019 was the costliest with regard to climate change and natural disasters. Damages and losses totaled some $3 trillion, more than $1 trillion greater than the prior decade.[5]

Public lands, recreation, and travel have also been adversely impacted by climate change. One troubling example is the US network of national parks. In mid-2021, the National Park Service issued a report—supported by two additional research papers—outlining new protocols for park managers in a time of escalating climate change. In essence, the directives afford ecologists and management guidelines to prioritize park oversight—what parts of a park they can try to save, what to adjust through shifting environmental change, and what to simply give up on. This triage-like approach acknowledges some parts of a park are going to disappear completely.[6]

Fig. 3.2. Photo by Nacho Canepa from Pexels.

Additionally, the COVID-19 pandemic has shed a stark light on the world community's capacity and ability to come together to mount a coordinated effort against a common enemy—for better or worse. Moving forward, given the interrelated dynamics of climate change, global cooperation at all levels will be essential to develop and implement any effective effort to stop and reverse dangerous climate issues. Again, should one part of the world stumble or refuse to take part in such an effort, consequences are likely to occur elsewhere—seen, for instance, in dust plumes from the Sahara Desert causing hazy skies and poor air quality in Omaha, Nebraska, in 2021.[7]

WATER, WATER . . . NOWHERE

I spent 36 years of my life in Los Angeles, and the weather was always predictable. Every summer we'd get wildfires in the Malibu Hills just northwest of the city; then by October the rains would hit, and that same embattled area would suffer massive flooding with many homes, ranches, and lives lost. Roughly seven years ago in 2014, the latest drought hit and with it, more wildfires. You'd see half the map of the state "on fire" during the nightly weather reports, even in farming areas in the middle of the state that were normally less affected by them. People selling their homes during this time actually hired companies to paint their lawns so they looked lush, green, and full. In reality, these lawns were dirt with patches of dying grass here and there . . . little tufts of green. Counties were put on rotating water usage schedules where residents could only water their properties on certain days of the week and for very short spans of time at that. Many Hollywood celebrities were called tone-deaf and even fined by the city because they paid premiums to have their lawns watered to maintain their beauty despite the drought and overall water shortages.

—Shelley Moench-Kelly

Climate change has also spotlighted a disturbing gender component. Estimates hold that roughly 80 percent of people displaced by climate change are women. Further, women are reportedly more than 14 times more likely to die during environmental disasters, given their roles as caregivers and often a lack of anything approaching financial independence, among other factors.[8]

The obvious gender imbalance of the effects of climate change are particularly acute in the developing world. Women compose the majority of the agricultural workforce in many countries and, as a result, endure particularly harsh consequences from extreme weather events that damage crops and harm livestock. This fact is especially true in countries where women lack equitable access to land and property rights.

Impact isn't solely segmented according to gender, though. Research has established a correlation between extreme temperature and precipitation in early life and educational attainment among children living in more tropical areas of the world. Higher than normal temperatures are connected with fewer years of schooling in Southeast Asia; likewise, excessive rainfall in a child's younger years harms educational achievement in Central America and the Caribbean. Moreover, in a rare departure from the usual dynamics of inequality, studies have found children from the most educated households experience the greatest educational penalties when exposed to hotter early-life conditions.[9]

CHANGE THAT HITS HOME

Climate change is something that's very near to me. I was born in the delta that sits between India and Nepal, at the foothills of the Himalayas. As the climate changes, there's a greater amount of ice meltdown in addition to massive cyclones, downpours, and wash-downs. Large swaths of ground have been shifting despite the government's ongoing effort to manage and limit the crisis as much as possible. In a 2021 article on the climate crisis's heavy toll on citizens of Bangladesh, author S. M. Najmus noted that "Bangladesh is a low-lying country having 19 coastal districts with a 42 million population, which are under threat due to climate change and the subsequent rise in sea level, cyclones, tidal surge, and permanent inundation, according to officials. Nearly 700,000 Bangladeshis were displaced on average each year over the last decade by natural disasters, said the Internal Displacement Monitoring Center [and] worryingly, some 13.3 million Bangladeshis could be displaced by 2050 following varied impacts of climate change."[10]

But not all hope is lost. These statistics have helped to create possible counteractivities explained in a 2021 *Bloomberg* article by Hadriana Lowenkrom that details the climate migration crisis caused by intensifying floods in Bangladesh. Dhaka is experiencing waves of displaced residents from low lying coastal zones each year: "We cannot absorb a potential 10 million climate refugees or climates that might occur over the next 10 to 20 years," [said] Saleemul Huq, director of the International Centre for Climate Change and Development. According to the *Bloomberg* article, Huq and his colleagues support creating migrant-friendly towns outside major cities to ease pressure on the overcrowded capital. This strategy can also be implemented in other countries. These locations would need to create and implement plans to address climate risks and economic opportunities to attract migrants, they wrote in a paper published in the journal *Science*. Selective relocation abroad is another, equally important solution, they said.[11]

Lowenkrom adds that Huq and his colleagues also wrote in this paper that these migrant-friendly towns should also have other attributes, such as being climate resilient as well as having a basic infrastructure in place. And because these refugees prefer not to move far from where they were displaced, these cities should foster cultural ethics and values of incoming migrants. This strategy is currently being implemented in at least five cities in Bangladesh.

—Faisal Hoque

Climate change has also highlighted a related education issue—the absence of people in leadership positions with sufficient education in, and exposure to, climate change to formulate policy and make decisions based on climate data. One example designed to help counteract this lack of appropriate skills lies in the Association of Climate Change Officers' initiative to boost training and credential programs. Other companies and organizations are likely to follow suit, as will high schools, colleges, and vocational training programs, especially in light of growing consumer influence over curricula deemed particularly relevant.

Further, there are increasing calls for more pervasive, low-carbon, sustainable development in a variety of industries and settings. In particular, experts see growth of "green skills" as a natural complement to the technological opportunities afforded by the Fourth Industrial Revolution. As we'll discuss later, the role of social entrepreneurs—those helping drive social change from bottom-up rather than from top-down dictums—can play a critical role in the growth and implementation of varied green skills and industries, as can use of quantum computing, artificial intelligence, and so-called geoengineering, large-scale, deliberate interventions in the planet's natural systems.

DIP A TOE, SEE CLIMATE CHANGE

Like my colleagues Faisal and Shelley, I've also had firsthand experiences regarding climate change. One such event has effectively occurred over the course of several decades. When I first came to attend school in Northern New England, day trips to the nearby ocean were a pervasive and popular way to relax and blow off some steam from studies. Then, however, those trips largely confined themselves to the beach itself, as the water was almost inevitably too cold to dip a foot in, let alone go swimming in. Some 40 years later, that's no longer the case. People now commonly go swimming in the same waters that were bone-chillingly cold back in the day. Granted, it's not like the water in the Caribbean or Mexico, but there's an undeniable rise in temperature that's palpable every time you step in the water—an experiential form of climate change education.

—Jeff Wuorio

Beyond the evident economic and educational ramifications, there is also increasing research that suggests that climate change can contribute to political and social instability.

Studies have shown that warmer temperatures and more frequent extreme weather events underscore a number of equally extreme conditions—such as violent crime and political unrest—that often culminate in organized violence and even outright revolution. For instance, one study conducted at the University of Colorado projected that instances of violent crime could jump by tens of thousands by the end of the century, depending on how quickly temperatures rise.[12]

A 2013 paper in the journal *Science* found that even the most seemingly innocuous change in temperature correlated with a 2.3 percent increase in interpersonal conflict rates and a 13.2 percent jump in group conflicts.[13] As the world continues to set records in temperature changes, rising sea levels, and other climate change benchmarks, it's by no means a major leap to establish a connection between those events and growing worldwide instability and violence.

Even current trends and recent events that have had a positive impact on slowing climate change stand to be temporary at best. One such issue is population. Worldwide, population growth has slowed dramatically. For instance, in the first release of results from the most recent census, the US population grew by just 7.4 percent, the second-slowest decade since the first census in 1790.

The United States is no outlier. Maternity wards in Europe are closing, and abandoned houses are being torn down for parkland. Universities
in South Korea are shutting down because of inadequate student enroll-
ment. With few exceptions, fertility rates worldwide are falling. Perhaps
even more striking, some projections hold that the world's population is
expected to virtually stop growing by the end of this century for the first
time in modern history.[14]

In one respect, that does address a longtime Achilles heel regarding
climate change action. Rapid population growth, accompanied by resulting industrialization, has long been associated with climate change. So
the reasoning goes, if fewer people occupy the planet, the less the effect
on climate.

A "HOTTER" SUN

I grew up in Taos, New Mexico, in the 1970s and always ran around
with a golden-bronze tan. Back then, we never worried about sun-
burn or skin cancer. If we got burned, Mom would slather us with
Noxzema . . . I can't stand the smell to this day! I moved away to
attend college in Los Angeles, where I stayed for more than 25 years.
Then my mother died early one summer, and I returned home. I spent
the day before her funeral with old friends and my brother, just visiting the beloved spots where we used to hang out. We must have
spent two hours around town and returned to our hotel at dusk. A
group of us met at the outdoor cantina and enjoyed a cooler evening,
but not before one of my friends told a joke and slapped me on the
wrist with glee. I felt a burning sensation and looked down to see
something I'd never seen before in my life: a cluster of what looked
like water blisters. The impact of his slap burst them wide open. They
were all tiny, like mustard seeds or pinheads, and they covered the
backs of both my wrists, just where my sleeves ended and the sun hit
my skin. I asked my brother, who'd been away from Taos just slightly

less time than me, if he had them, and he did, even more so because he wore a tank top. We discussed it later and, while we have no proof, agreed that the sun felt hotter against our skin and we suffered more than when we did as kids. Our other friends and family had stayed local all those years and bore no reactions. We could only attribute it to climate change, maybe a larger hole in the ozone? That reaction nailed climate change home for me and my brother. We're advocates for change now, whereas before "the blister incident," neither of us really took it seriously.

—S. M., Veterinarian, Los Angeles, CA

Unfortunately, reality is not quite so simple. For one thing, researchers point out that smaller populations would likely do little to counteract what climate damage has already taken place. While a large population is an element of overall climate change, researchers insist that smaller populations are not the climate change "silver bullet" that some suggest.[15] Further, it's not so much an issue of the number of people as it is individual behavior. In so many words, people do not "emit" equally—one person's effect on climate is likely to differ quite a bit from others'. The overall number of people involved tends to matter less.

A similar dynamic exists with the recent shift—driven largely by the COVID-19 pandemic—to remote work and similar options. Although climate scientists have documented drops in carbon emissions due to work at home and other arrangements involving less travel, once again the benefit will certainly have a short shelf life if work shifts back primarily to an in-person system. Here, the jury remains out. Although many workers have expressed support for continued flexible work options and some companies and organizations have made public commitments to just that, others are keeping their cards very close to their vests. What will take place in post-COVID-19 relaxed health standards—and to what extent any meaningful change stays in place with regard to varied work and employment options—remains to be seen.

Even countries attempting to adopt meaningful climate reduction measures are facing significant and often surprising challenges. Recent events in France illustrate this. In May 2021, the French National Assembly approved a comprehensive climate bill covering varied forms of French life. Among other elements, the legislation would mandate more vegetarian meals at state-funded canteens and curb any efforts to expand existing French airports. Polluters could be charged with "ecocide," an environmental damage crime carrying prison terms of up to 10 years.[16] Climate change measures would be added to the French constitution itself.

Although the measures have drawn the usual opposition from major corporations that allege such measures could seriously harm the nation's economy, environmental groups have also come out in opposition. They say the measures simply don't go far enough and represent capitulation to France's powerful business federations.

Ultimately, many feel that it will require a significant upswell of public support for climate change mitigation policies to drive truly significant effort to combat climate change.

In particular, according to certain research, Americans will likely be more supportive of government efforts to fight climate change if the issue is framed in a somewhat specific manner.

A 2020 report by the Washington, DC-based nonprofit organization Resources of the Future identified several surprising conclusions on how people view the issue of climate change. Perhaps most eye-opening was the study's finding that people were most supportive of climate change action when they were concerned about its impact on future generations. This form of "sociotropic" reasoning—awareness of and concern for interpersonal relationships—elicited far greater enthusiasm for climate change action than other outcomes, such as the economic toll. Education on climate change's influence in more widespread floods and wildfires was also pinpointed as another catalyst for backing significant climate change action.[17]

Another possible factor in boosting public support for climate change policy is educating the public about the inherent conservative bent of many climate studies and projections. In so many words, while climate skeptics argue that perhaps the effects of climate change won't be as disastrous as some studies forecast, many climate researchers emphasize that, in fact, many of their projections don't go far enough when speculating about the consequences of climate change. As John Harte, a professor of environmental science at the University of California at Berkeley, has noted, "We often hear criticism of global warming science from non-scientists who like to point out that there's uncertainty in the climate models, and that maybe the effect won't be as bad as we project. But what this scientific experiment is showing us is that, if anything, our current climate models are underestimating the magnitude of future warming."[18]

Despite all this grim news, justifiable reason for optimism does exist. Public support for significant action to fight climate change continues to grow. According to a 2020 Pew Research Center survey, broad majorities of the public say they would support a number of initiatives to reduce the impacts of climate change, such as large-scale tree-planting efforts, tax credits for businesses that capture carbon emissions, and tougher fuel efficiency standards for vehicles. In an era where bipartisanship seems a quaint memory, that support comes from more than half of Republicans and an even greater number of Democrats.[19]

Further, the technological possibilities and opportunities of the Fourth Industrial Revolution afford potential tools and solutions outside the purview of policy and regulation. From more effective monitoring of air quality to decarbonization of varied industries to using big data and blockchain-based solutions to encourage environmentally friendly consumer and business decision-making, the Fourth Industrial Revolution (4IR) could transform the overall effort to curb climate change through solutions focused on transformation and not mere deprivation or shifts in individual behavior.

That will all depend to a certain degree on the public's clear understanding of what 4IR is and can genuinely do, rather than draconian warnings of robots taking control of our lives out of human hands. That and other misleading conclusions like it are another prevalent form of disruption—misinformation—that will be addressed in the following chapter.

CHAPTER 3—LEARN AND TRANSFORM

1. The internet, social media, and other forms of immediate information and communication have served to boost more widespread exposure to—and empathy for—the catastrophic consequences of climate change, an element of "sociotropic" reasoning cited earlier. That, suggest some researchers, can be critical in boosting efforts toward more aggressive climate change policy and action. The greater the number of people who see and genuinely understand that climate change is real and is growing exponentially more problematic, the greater the call for meaningful steps. Hopefully, it will foster a far different mindset from one of climate change being somebody else's problem.

2. More immediate and immersive forms of news and information are providing a more personal, experiential form of learning with regard to climate change. One such example is a video produced by the United Nations Environment Program that allows viewers an immersive, virtual experience of how everyday choices can contribute to or counteract climate change, from food packaging to forgoing automobile trips in favor of other means of transportation. These and other tools allow people throughout the world to see and learn firsthand, further establishing the sense of personal impact that's so essential to boosting climate change action.

3. Greater awareness of the impact of climate change mandates a systematic, comprehensive strategy to leverage that shift to the utmost. Here, it can be helpful to subdivide the global topic of planning and execution into two different categories. First is mitigation—those steps that can be taken to minimize and even reverse environmental damage, including retrofitting buildings to lesson environmental impact and leverage clean energy, developing more sustainable transportation, greater overall use of solar and hydroelectric power, and other actions. The second category is adaptation—policies and actions with which to adjust to the realities of climate change. These include preparing for longer and more active fire seasons, updating community disaster plans in anticipation of more severe weather, and other proactive steps that both acknowledge and prepare for climate change events. This two-pronged approach acknowledges the reality that climate change cannot be limited just to corrective action—it also underscores the fact that climate change isn't going to be solved overnight and that proactive planning is necessary to minimize existing damage as much as possible.

CHAPTER 4

MISINFORMATION

THE FILM *A PERFECT STORM* captured the catastrophic consequences of a fishing boat caught in a confluence of deadly weather. However unlikely, these factors came together to produce a once-in-a-lifetime storm. It was all too real.

The problem of misinformation is a perfect storm in its own right. Given technology's capacity to deliver and share "news" of all sorts, people can now be bombarded with a constant hail of information—so-called infostorms. Further, a variety of factors can prompt infostorm recipients to accept what they're seeing and hearing as absolute truth, whether it be data on the COVID-19 pandemic or information about a company or organization's financial health.

However, so much of what we all can embrace as fact is anything but true. But, like a real storm, the consequences of intentional misinformation are devastating—and they may only be growing worse and more pervasive.

Fig. 4.1. Photo by Austin Distel on Unsplash.

Although the idea of intentionally spreading misleading or invented facts came to prominence in the 2016 American presidential election, the idea is hardly new. One well-known example with some miles on it has to do with the explosion of the battleship *Maine* in Havana Harbor in the late 19th century. With no evidence save for sheer jingoism, American newspapers blamed Cuban terrorists for causing the deadly explosion. The Spanish-American War followed not long thereafter.

APRIL FOOLS!

It's not news to me that misinformation and fake news have been around for quite a while. I was completely taken in by one such ruse, albeit a harmless one, back in 1985. The April 1 edition of *Sports Illustrated* included a lengthy story called "The Curious Case of Sidd Finch." Written by George Plimpton, the story detailed the "discovery" of a baseball pitcher who, it was alleged, could throw the ball at more than 160 miles an hour. The wunderkind rookie working out with the New York Mets also only wore one shoe—a hiking boot—and had traveled to Tibet to learn "yogic mastery of mind and body." He was reportedly torn between a career in the big leagues or playing the French horn professionally. I bought the entire story, as did many Mets fans who rejoiced at the prospect of such a superhuman player (reportedly several general managers of professional teams asked to obtain more information about Finch).

The beauty of the scam, as it is with any "successful" form of misinformation, was in the details. The Mets organization cooperated, even providing Finch with a locker between two noteworthy "real" players. The story was accompanied by photographs supposedly of Finch (he was played by a friend of the photographer for the story who, as it happened, was tall and sported size 14 shoes), with Finch carefully positioned in every shot so that his face wasn't totally visible. The Mets' pitching coach appeared in photographs alongside Finch, offering advice and feedback.

On April 15, the truth was revealed. It was pointed out that the subhead to the story read, "He's a pitcher, part yogi and part recluse. Impressively liberated from our opulent life-style, Sidd's deciding about yoga—and his future in baseball." Extracting the first letter from each of those words creates the phrase "Happy April Fool's Day—a(h) fib." I don't think I've ever felt more gullible in my life.

—Jeff Wuorio

More recently, false reports during the 2017 French presidential election alleged that Emmanuel Macron had established several offshore bank accounts.[1] Using the hashtag #MacronGate, some 7,000 Twitter users quickly distributed images of two documents that supposedly identified Macron as the owner of an offshore account in the Caribbean. Although the reports were quickly and thoroughly debunked, it's difficult to imagine that the intended impact of the misinformation was also thoroughly eliminated. After all, once something is seen, it can be very difficult to unsee it.

But misinformation is anything but purely political. The recent COVID-19 pandemic provides ample evidence. From the idea that consuming bleach can kill the virus to the still-breathing "theory" that the virus was created in a laboratory as a biological weapon, the COVID-19 pandemic has generated a flurry of misinformation. In fact, a report in the August 10, 2020, edition of the *American Journal of Tropical Medicine and Hygiene* estimated that the pandemic has fostered more than 2,300 conspiracy theories, rumors, and other forms of misinformation.[2] Sadly, that's more than just a matter of confusion and misinformation. The researchers of the new study found that COVID-19-related rumors were linked to thousands of hospitalizations and hundreds of deaths.

In circumstances such as the COVID-19 pandemic, widespread misinformation goes well beyond the embrace of inaccurate and potentially dangerous material. In so doing, many who latch on to falsehoods also tend to reject the advice and information offered by established experts and reliable sources. The reaction, known by researchers as "reactance"—an analysis developed by psychologist Jack Brehm in the mid-1960s—refers to the idea that when individual freedoms are lowered or even threatened to be reduced, people are naturally driven to try to recapture what they've lost or are convinced they're going to. In the case of COVID-19, the more authorities encouraged mask wearing, social distancing, and other measures, the more likely many people were to do the exact opposite.

Respected experts in their fields aren't the only ones to suffer from a perceived lack of credibility due to misinformation. Media as a whole has come under suspicion as well. According to a recent study, almost half of the nearly 6,000 American college students surveyed said they lacked confidence in discerning real from fake news on social media. And 36 percent of them said the threat of misinformation made them trust all media less.[3]

That distrust carries over to their elders. Numerous studies have suggested that people worldwide who've been exposed to disinformation and fake news tend to apply a general level of skepticism to all media outlets, including many of the oldest and most established. While expressing concern over the ramifications of that absence of trust, one *Wall Street Journal* columnist quipped that "most of these organizations now rank in public trust a little below emailed pleas from deposed Nigerian princes."[4] To further emphasize the point, recent polls have pinpointed Americans' trust in mainstream media at historic lows.

"REPORTS OF MY DEATH"

I am on the Baby Boomer–Gen Xer cusp and have many younger friends and colleagues. Over the years, I've had to ask them to fact-check their information before blindly posting it on social media. For example, a dancer friend posted in mid-2021 about the devastating, unexpected death of dancer Gregory Hines. Her post began with a plaintive "OH NOOO!" and I had to do a double take, because somewhere in my memory I remembered he died at 54 years old . . . and not in 2021! Additionally, her post made me question myself. Here is where I think society's acceptance of fake news begins. If you, like I, question the source and proceed to investigate further, you'll eventually discover what's fact and what's fiction. If not, then we exist on a flat Earth and COVID-19 is a hoax. Sure enough, Mr. Hines passed in 2003, but my friend apparently didn't read far enough into her source to notice this and just posted her reaction immediately. Close to 50 of her friends responded with sadness, disbelief, and sorrow. Not one of them corrected her; they all just took her for her word. I gently commented that his death was as devastating when it happened in 2003 as it was on this day, its 18th anniversary. Several of her friends chided me for being a "know-it-all," a "buzz-kill," and even a "Karen," certainly none of which were my intent. This example is relatively benign but shows the power of how quickly misinformation can spread.

—Shelley Moench-Kelly

Still, it begs the question why so many people readily believe all sorts of misinformation, some of which can seem ludicrously inaccurate or exaggerated to many others. One possible explanation is what might be referred to as "expedient laziness." Presented with news or information that often requires corroboration, many might groan at the thought of plowing through other sources and sifting through claims and counter-claims. Instead, it's far easier and faster simply to ask others what they think—a relatively quick way to build confidence that something is, in fact, true—while gaining a degree of social acceptance by simply going along with the crowd.

SAY IT, THEN LIVE WITH IT

The next time you are ready to post something on your favorite social media platform, remember that there are no takebacks on the internet. Your digital footprint will increasingly carry far more weight—perhaps even more than your résumé.

The recent poster child for bad behavior on the social media front serves as yet another example of how quickly one can find themselves in hot water with just a few screen taps.[5]

This time, *Guardians of the Galaxy* director James Gunn was fired by Disney for making jokes about pedophilia and rape on Twitter.[6] "I used to make a lot of offensive jokes," Gunn said via Twitter. "I don't anymore. I don't blame my past self for this, but I like myself more and feel like a more full human being and creator today."[7]

Gunn isn't alone. Across most industries, we're seeing just how tricky it can be to navigate the intersection of career and social media. Just one politically incorrect statement on Facebook, one combative tweet, or one offensive Instagram photo can create a virtual maelstrom of trouble. The World Economic Forum (WEF) says building and managing a healthy identity (both online and offline) with integrity, understanding the nature of digital footprints (and their real-life consequences) and managing them responsibly, and being empathetic toward one's own and others' needs and feelings online are three of the best ways to teach children how to have positive digital footprints.

As adults, we could all learn a thing or two from this youth-focused advice from the WEF. Namely, how to conduct ourselves online in an era where many high-profile individuals are instead choosing to take the "low" road.

Four Positive Principles to Follow

Each time you post a tweet, upload a photo to Facebook, or share content online, remember, the internet literally never forgets—any inappropriate photos, poorly thought-out comments, or questionable content becomes part of your digital footprint.

There are no "takebacks" in social media, where even an errant tweet that's quickly deleted can be screenshotted and shared with the world within seconds. Whether you are a student or the head of a 5,000-employee enterprise, leading responsibly in the era of social media requires a focused, conscientious approach that's rooted in these four principles:

POST WITH EMPATHY

Empathy—the action of understanding, being innately aware of, being sensitive to, and/or vicariously undergoing the feelings, thoughts, and experiences of another of either the past or present—is particularly valuable during periods of disruption or uncertainty. That's because empathy helps us be approachable, stokes open dialogue, and encourages high levels of sharing. A dose of empathy goes a long way in the world of social media, where the audience is both broad and diverse. Putting yourself in someone else's shoes can open up new lines of communication, create new levels of understanding, and help everyone achieve common goals.

He needs no introduction, and it's no secret that the Dalai Lama is one leader whose contributions are highly inclusive by nature. It's no different on Facebook. On July 16, 2018, he posted the following:

continued

> "Just as we can learn how helpful love and
> compassion can be, we can come to understand
> that anger, pride, jealousy, and arrogance
> can be detrimental. We can also learn to distinguish
> arrogant pride, looking down on others, from
> the useful pride that is involved in boosting
> our confidence."

BE INCLUSIVE

An intention or policy of including people who might otherwise be excluded or marginalized—an inclusive approach—goes a long way on social media, where being open to diverse perspectives is imperative. Twitter, Facebook, and other platforms can also help bring awareness to our diversity and our intent for inclusivity.

With 17.7 million followers, Pope Francis has a lot of eyeballs waiting for his next tweet, most of which simply ooze inclusivity, such as the following from July 7, 2018:

> "May all humanity hear the cry of the children
> of the Middle East. Drying their tears the world
> will get back it's [sic] dignity."

ALWAYS GO FOR THE HIGH MORAL GROUND

There's a time and a place for arguing and defending your ground, and social media isn't it. Getting into arguments in the virtual setting—where all eyes can see who's saying what to whom—doesn't fly. Aim for the higher ground by always maintaining a professional tone and keep the backbiting and insult throwing out of the conversation.

Politics in America is a deeply polarizing, divisive topic today, but Harvard Business School professor and former Medtronic CEO Bill George uses his articles to address touchy topics in a diplomatic way:

> Much has been written about the harm that President Donald Trump's trade wars will do to American farmers, manufacturers, and their employees. That is all true. But the real losers in this "America First" initiative will be American consumers. If President Trump follows through on his threats, US consumers will see rapid rises in the prices of everything from T-shirts to automobiles to new homes.[8]

DISPLAY COURAGE

As with all situations, everything can't be good all the time. But people will naturally look to others for guidance and support in both the good and the bad times. Don't be afraid to challenge the status quo, share your mission, set boundaries, and/or stand behind your values.

With 350,000-plus Twitter followers and an active presence across numerous social media platforms, actress Ashley Judd boldly stands up for causes such as the #MeToo movement and human rights. On May 29, 2018, she tweeted the following:

"Delighted and really looking forward to brilliant scoop and perspective about #humanrights issues and solutions, as I attend my first @CarrCenter for Human Rights board meetings as a member for the board. Always great to be back at my alma mater @Kennedy_School, too! #harvard"

The next time you pull up your favorite social media platform online, remember that everything you do there will impact you and everyone around you.

continued

> Just as you'd avoid a bar fight or a road rage incident in the real
> world, it is important to keep your image and reputation in mind in
> the virtual world. Let us use social media for what it was intended: to
> "engage" with others, keep people informed, share knowledge, and
> create open communications.
>
> —Faisal Hoque

As tech journalist John Battelle told *The New York Times*, "We are living online, but have yet to fully realize the implications of doing so. One of those implications is that our tracks through the digital sand are eternal."[9]

Somewhat understandable, but nevertheless a potentially explosive dynamic. For one, misinformation is simply becoming more and more widespread. For example, in a 2017 study in the *Journal of Economic Perspectives*, which studied false news in the 2016 presidential election, of 1,208 US adults surveyed, 15 percent said they remembered seeing false news stories. Further, 8 percent admitted to seeing one of these stories and believing it.[10]

More recently, in March 2020, it was reported that nearly 30 percent of US adults believed the Chinese government created COVID-19 as a bioweapon.[11] In an additional study published a month later, 25 percent said they believed the outbreak was intentionally planned by authorities.[12]

Additionally, misinformation is fast upping its game in terms of its persuasiveness. No longer limited to the dissemination of fake stories and so-called information, the "next generation" of fake news has arrived. Now, audio and video created and altered to accompany and boost content can make disinformation seem all the more legitimate—and more difficult to disprove. Even people unskilled in computer technology can use free, easy-to-use apps to do everything from swapping out one face for another to mimic certain facial features, to cloning speech patterns to produce fake audio that sounds just like a real person.

Some app makers have become concerned about their products' capacity to deceive. Some have reportedly been sufficiently dismayed that they've hesitated to release full versions of some of their technology, for concern about the damage they could create in the wrong hands. (Can you imagine such an app falling into the clutches of Lex Luthor, Dr. Evil, or some other like supervillain? What if that app fell into the hands of a real-life corrupt politician or criminal?)

Even fake news meant to entertain has become so polished that entire governments and news agencies have been occasionally taken in. For instance, in 2012, the satirical newspaper *The Onion* ran a story that proclaimed North Korean leader Kim Jong-Un the "sexiest man alive in 2012." It seemed genuine enough to prompt the online version of China's *People Daily* to reprint portions of the story, citing in particular Kim's "air of power that masks an unmistakable cute, cuddly side," his "impeccable fashion sense, chic short hairstyle," as well as "that famous smile."[13]

While, for Americans at least, the proliferation of fake news' contribution to the deadly January 6, 2021, uprising against the federal government remains the most vivid example, other elements of society have been targeted by misinformation—with devastating outcomes. Companies such as Fitbit and Avon have been hit with false reports of planned buyouts to impact stock prices.[14] Even iconic companies such as Coca-Cola have had to cope with concocted news, such as one story that alleged that Dasani water bottles contained parasites.[15]

It would be understandable to assume that the associated costs of combatting and counteracting disinformation would be substantial, and that assumption would be correct. According to a 2019 study by Israel-based cybersecurity firm CHEQ and the University of Baltimore, fake news in its varied forms is costing the global economy some $78 billion a year. A sampling of a breakdown of that amount identifies economic losses from health misinformation ($9 billion annually), financial misinformation ($17 billion), reputation management ($9 billion), platform safety programs and efforts ($3 billion), and loss of brand dollars advertising next to fake news ($235 million).[16]

Misinformation has also impacted health care in ways other than financially. When then-president Barack Obama first proposed widespread health-care reform, a concomitant suggestion posited elsewhere was the idea that elderly people would have to consult with "death panels" to discuss end-of-life options such as euthanasia. These rumors started with statements made by former New York lieutenant governor Betsy McCaughey but quickly spread to conservative media outlets, as well as prominent members of the Republican Party.[17] The concocted crisis was further sharpened with an accompanying false rumor that older people were to be "judged" according to their continuing value to society as a whole.

The entire controversy is mindbogglingly absurd in retrospect, but, nonetheless, a substantial number of Americans thought the news legitimate, at least in part. A poll conducted by the Pew Center in August 2009 found that 30 percent of the public thought the "death panel" rumor was true, with another 20 percent unsure of the legitimacy of the statement.[18]

While death panels were nothing more than a concocted panic, misinformation can also compromise public safety and reaction to genuine crises. Subsequent research following the landfall of Hurricane Sandy in 2012 found more than 10,000 tweets containing fake images of the hurricane. It's not difficult to speculate that distribution of this false information could have led to poor understanding of the severity of the storm, as well as potentially inadequate or misguided safety precautions. Just as troubling was the finding that the overwhelming number of Sandy-related false tweets were retweets—testimony to the disinformation muscle that relatively few people can command by sharing falsehoods with those likely to push them further down the line.[19]

Fig. 4.2. Photo by Michal Mation on Unsplash.

RESPOND, OR ELSE

Maybe 15–20 years ago, there were scam emails circulating from "Nigerian royalty" that peppered our inboxes requesting green cards in exchange for money or even proposing marriage to gain US citizenship. Others out and out asked for money without a reciprocal exchange. Even my 80-something-year-old mother knew they were scams and would call me in fits of laughter as they became more frequent and ridiculous. But over the last decade, those scams have bilked I'm sure millions of dollars from unsuspecting victims because now they're disguised with the presence of threats and fear. "If you don't pay us $500 by Tuesday at noon, you could lose your health insurance," or "Please call us immediately regarding your Social Security benefits or risk losing them." The system has become so elaborate and real-looking that unless you do your due diligence before responding to them, you could easily become a victim. The moral of the story is, be careful, be prepared, and if you can't prove something is real, don't fall victim to it!

—B. G., Banker, Orange, CA

Young people can be particularly vulnerable to fake news. For one thing, given their youth and lack of experience relative to their elders, young people are naturally more prone to believing what they see without taking any steps to determine legitimacy. Since their emotional management is less developed, they're particularly susceptible to the sorts of emotional appeals that fake news tries to leverage. Moreover, even though young people, having been raised with technology, might appear to be more tech savvy, that ability doesn't carry over to being able to separate real news from fake.

That conclusion is supported by research. A report from researchers at Stanford University's Graduate School of Education found a troubling inability to reason about what information students discovered on the internet. In particular, students struggled to separate legitimate news from advertising or sponsored content or to understand the actual source of the information they were reading.[20]

Fortunately, there's a rising effort to help students better delineate between genuine information and fake news. Programs addressing media literacy have been established at all educational levels to train students on what to do to verify what they see online. Alarmed by the proliferation of false content online, lawmakers around the country are pushing schools to put more emphasis on teaching students how to tell fact from fiction.

Nor do such programs have to be particularly time-consuming. Research from the Reboot Foundation found that interventions as simple as reading a short article or watching a three-and-a-half-minute-long educational video on spotting fake news can make an immediate difference in test subjects' abilities to pinpoint erroneous material of all sorts.[21]

In a rare bright spot, the COVID-19 pandemic has helped fuel legislative action against fake news throughout the world. From Algeria to Vietnam, a number of countries passed "fake news" regulations during the COVID-19 outbreak, with additional actions ranging from media literacy efforts to government-sponsored programming geared to educating the public about misinformation.

But perhaps the greatest risk that misinformation carries is a potentially destructive synergy with the other three drivers of change discussed in this book—COVID-19, climate change, and the Fourth Industrial Revolution. In so many words, opportunities inherent in those disruptors revolve to a large degree around how well misinformation—fake news designed to confuse and portray itself as fact—can be identified, discredited, and eliminated as much as possible.

Misinformation targeting COVID-19 has already been discussed. From utterly unsubstantiated "cures" to insidious conspiracies, the pandemic has graphically shown how deadly misinformation can be. In the first three months of 2020 alone, nearly 6,000 people worldwide were hospitalized because of coronavirus misinformation, recent research suggests. During this time frame, researchers say at least 800 people may have died due to misinformation related to COVID-19.[22]

One of the most destructive forms of recent misinformation has to do with COVID-19—specifically, pushing lies and other falsehoods about life-saving vaccinations. Although as I write this the struggle against the pandemic is still ongoing, it can be helpful to review several examples of COVID-19 "news" that were anything but legitimate. They can prove useful in helping to identify patterns of misinformation, about COVID-19 as well as other issues:

- COVID-19 vaccines will change people's DNA. The video by osteopath Carrie Madej earned some 300,000 views.[23]

- False claims that the COVID-19 vaccination contains microchips that can be used to track and control people.

- False claims that the vaccine causes infertility or death.

- Outrageous claims, often "attributed" to people of notoriety such as Bill Gates, acknowledging that vaccines will inevitably kill hundreds of thousands.

These and other examples contain a number of common elements. One is the objective of promoting panic—an emotion that can inevitably hinder rational thought and reasoning. Another is a connection with celebrities—after all, since they're famous, they must know what they're talking about. And last is an insidious charge that people may have trouble recognizing in themselves, such as microchips and damage to genetic structure.

Fake news about the "consequences" of the Fourth Industrial Revolution may not be quite so stark and fatal, but the aftereffects stand to be irrefutably damaging. Concocted stories about the robots "taking over" and shoving human workers to the sidelines stand to divert attention from the actual challenges faced by the workforce of the future—to be better trained and better equipped to leverage the advantages that spreading technology can offer.

So far as misinformation regarding climate change, in the eyes of many, the damage has already been done. In a paper published in *WIREs Climate Change*, British scientists labeled fake news about climate change as perhaps the biggest target of any sort of organized misinformation campaign. Citing its ability to perpetuate climate change skepticism, denial, and contrarianism, the report tracks the journey of misinformation, including funding from fossil fuel interests to its spread fueled by misinformation's knack for leveraging confirmation bias and other psychological characteristics.[24]

Ultimately, the overriding challenge facing society is the vital importance of rebuilding trust in fact-based, objective decision-making, be it regarding technology, public health issues, or a planet that continues its exponential warming. Only then will the vast opportunities embedded in these dynamic forces of change be fully realized. And the stakes of capturing that opportunity as fully as possible are very, very high.

CHAPTER 4–LEARN AND TRANSFORM

1. Experiential learning can prove central to better educating people of all ages about misinformation and ways to identify it. Rather than just hearing about fake news after it's been uncovered, experiential learning—such as quizzes and other tools where readers are asked to select which is real and which is not—can equip people of all backgrounds to proactively look for certain types of phrases, wording, and other signs that the information they're seeing may not be genuine. Particularly valuable for school-age children, education in media literacy can bolster critical-thinking skills, understanding point of view, and other important talents central to a world that has and will be characterized by change.

2. Whether within the confines of formal education or personal skill development, systemic thinking is absolutely essential to the growth of greater media literacy. Although there are many strategies and questions to ask when identifying potential misinformation, some core ideas to bear in mind are as follows:

    a. What is the source of the information? Is it an established news medium or an anonymous source?

    b. What techniques are being used to make the message credible or believable? Does it have statistics from a reputable, known source? Does it contain quotes from a subject expert?

    c. Are attributions specific to people or other reliable sources, or do phrases such as "reports suggest" hint that there's nothing genuinely credible about where the information came from?

    d. Are certain details omitted? For instance, in an obituary, does the article lack cause of death? Although these are frequently left out to protect privacy, credible sources generally add the phrase "no cause of death was given" or some other explanation.

    e. How did the information make you feel? Angry? Upset? Confused? Do you think that was the author's actual intent?

Questions like these and others can point readers toward an article, video, or other piece's legitimacy—or lack thereof.

3. Approach misinformation and fake news with a sense of empathy toward others—not for people attempting to pull off such scams but for others who may be unwittingly taken in by misleading or potentially dangerous falsehoods. If you spot what you believe to be false news, call them out on it. Let the person posting the material know that you believe it to be false and cite your reasoning for doing so. Cite the questions and other means of investigation you used to identify the ersatz posting. Treat those who believe the fake news with an understanding of how easy it can be to fall for such mischief.

4. Another weapon against misinformation and fake news is fact-checking websites. These provide a quick and accurate way of investigating all sorts of media that come across as suspicious. They include the following:

    a. AP Fact Check, Associated Press

    b. Factcheck.org

    c. PolitiFact

    d. *The Washington Post*'s Fact Checker

    e. Flackcheck.org

SECTION TWO

AMID THE CHANGE, ALL THIS OPPORTUNITY

THE AUTHOR LEO TOLSTOY once noted, "Everyone thinks of changing the world, but no one thinks of changing himself."

Pervasive, fast-moving change can lend the feeling of being out of control, that something other than our own free will is calling the shots. And, given the change that the entire planet has experienced of late—and is going to experience moving forward—it's understandable that many feel as though something else is in the driver's seat.

The COVID-19 pandemic that is now (somewhat) on the wane is an ideal example. More than a year of fear and uncertainty, punctuated by newfound expressions such as "social distancing" and "shelter in place," can naturally promote a hunker-down mentality of doing little more than keeping your head down and riding things out. For most of us, there seemed little else we could do.

The Fourth Industrial Revolution can have a similar feel. While not as extreme or, frankly, irrational as a "robots are taking over" level of panic, the wave of exponential change can nonetheless feel precisely like a wave—a sweeping force that repeatedly washes over and transforms most everything in its path. And, just like a wave, the only thing it feels as though any of us can do is to either let it carry us along or try to stay out of its way.

Happily, that's not the case at all. Rather than seeing all this change as something frightening and even destructive, those who take the time to identify—and act on—the enormous and widespread opportunity inherent in disruption will truly fulfill their growing roles as individual leaders. That's because opportunity is most everywhere, with the potential to change our economy; business and working lives; education; and a number of other areas—and all for the better.

It begins with the individual. While corporations, governments, educational systems, and other entities stand poised to benefit from change, disruption has placed the individual at the heart of much of that change. Not only can individuals leverage change for their own benefit, but they can also impact change at much higher levels than ever before.

But, as is the case with all forms of opportunity amid all this change, certain critical components have to be in place to leverage all sorts of opportunity to the furthest degree possible. First on the list—once again—is empathy. Rather than the cold quid pro quo of transactional relationships, empathy has been shown to boost productivity, a willingness to collaborate, and an eagerness to go above and beyond. That holds true for all types of groups, from the largest company to the smallest community volunteer group—in fact, in most every type of relationship you can imagine.

Opportunity also mandates systemic thinking, careful planning, and subsequent action to take good intentions and make them viable and effective. Setting specific goals and objectives, establishing time frames, creating effective organizational structure, and other steps are critical to build on the foundation of empathy to position individuals, as well as groups, to leverage the opportunity that widespread change holds.

Lastly, use experiential learning at every opportunity. Remember, the change in the world that we're experiencing right now is unprecedented—when it comes to understanding what is really happening and how you can best fit in, long-standing rules are few and far between. Feel free to experiment, and encourage others to do the same. Tap into your sense of empathy and go easy on yourself and others when the experiment doesn't work out as planned. Experiential learning with an open mind is essential to make the coming years as constructive and rewarding as possible.

CHAPTER 5

INDIVIDUAL OPPORTUNITY—
THE NEWLY EMPOWERED

A QUOTE OFTEN ATTRIBUTED to the anthropologist Margaret Mead states, "Never doubt that a small group of thoughtful, committed citizens can change the world. Indeed, it's the only thing that ever has." Given the convergence of the four forces that are driving sweeping change everywhere on the planet, that observation may now be truer than ever. As much as anywhere else, the collision of the four drivers of change— the Fourth Industrial Revolution, COVID-19, climate change, and misinformation—offer unprecedented opportunity to the individual. That's because, from a global standpoint, much of the enormous change that has already occurred, as well as change that has yet to come, has focused on empowering the individual and making him or her better informed, more engaged, and hopefully happier, healthier, and more fulfilled.

Individuals have more opportunity than ever to direct the course of their own lives, be it in a professional or career setting, education, health care, or many other areas. We are all becoming leaders in our own right, empowered to make decisions, adapt to the changing environment around us, and serve as catalysts for pervasive change for the better.

If there's a single word that encapsulates the opportunity afforded to these individual leaders, it might well be *consumer*. No matter if it's related to work, health care, or varied forms of collective, community involvement, the individual has been moved to the powerful role of consumer—the end user who wields the capacity and influence to impact and transform.

Fig. 5.1. Photo by Ian Stauffer on Unsplash.

With regard to work, individuals will have increasing opportunities to leverage technology and shifting managerial priorities to gain more varied training and work experience. Through revisiting and adopting new organizational principles, individuals will also have access to different work experiences and the opportunity to accumulate a broader array of marketable skills.

While companies may deem the pandemic a hard pill to swallow because they're used to closely monitoring employees in-house, in reality it has given employees the opportunity to potentially become more productive. According to Great Place to Work, 5 percent of American employees worked from home pre-pandemic, but by May 2020, more than 60 percent were working remotely.[1] And that group working in varied alternate settings has made the most of their time, according to a study by Stanford University of some 16,000 workers whose productivity when working from home increased by 13 percent. The study attributed the boost to a quieter work environment and fewer breaks and days lost to illness.[2]

This "altered reality" of remote workers offers formerly office-trapped employees certain freedoms, freedoms that include self-management, training, and work experience. Freelancers are used to being a CEO, human resources, and employee "superworker" in their own jobs because there's no one to report to until a client hires them. What freelancers call a "gig economy" has now spread to office workers worldwide.

It also provides the opportunity for new remote workers to gain additional skills and managerial expertise, which, in turn, makes them more marketable. If a company doesn't value its employees and/or is pressuring them to work in-house even if they fear possible exposure to the pandemic or do not wish to spend hours commuting every day, there are companies ready and willing to hire those employees as remote workers, especially with their newfound skills. The employee, rather than the company, has the upper hand in deciding when and how they wish to work.

Another component of remote work is the discovery and understanding that not every worker produces best in a standard nine-to-five environment. Some people are night owls; others are morning people. As a result, perfectly capable employees who thrive at night might be incorrectly classified as slow, lazy, or incapable of doing a job that just so happens to fall into their nonproductive times of the day. Writers, for example, generally thrive in quiet surroundings and less so in chaotic or typical "office" environments with noise, interruptions, and meetings.

Remote work affords the scheduling autonomy that allows employees to work at a time of day when their skills are at their optimal. No matter if that's early in the morning, in the middle of the night, or at intermittent points throughout the day, workers are gaining the independence necessary to use the day to their advantage rather than adhering to a needlessly unproductive schedule.

Fig. 5.2. Photo by RODNAE Productions from Pexels.

Additionally, individuals will have the opportunity to develop what can be referred to as greater self-management skills. With greater autonomy from traditional, hierarchical management styles and structure, individual workers (particularly the growing population of freelancers) will have the chance and the impetus to develop such softer skills as active learning, resilience, stress tolerance, and flexibility. They'll assume that much more control as leaders of their own careers.

GOOD NEWS: WE LOVE TO LEARN!

Forget what you've heard about old dogs and new tricks. Even if it were true—and it isn't—it wouldn't help you out. The fact is that you'll need to adapt in order to thrive in the future workplace. And the good news is that our minds are wired with an unquenchable desire to learn, whether we recognize it or not.

To help you tap into your learning potential, keep these three fundamental questions on standby—and revisit them whenever you start feeling worried that your skills or knowledge might be getting stale.[3]

1. Am I stuck in a rut?

Sometimes it can be hard to tell, unless you take a step back to consider it. Think about any habits or patterns you've fallen into: Do they feel tedious, dull, and less productive than they could be? Do your work routines feel hard to change, even if you wanted to? Take a hard look at daily, weekly, and monthly to-do lists: Are you doing the same things over and over again, but not making career progress? Are you talking to the same people, doing the same tasks, and sitting at the same desk day after day?

Picking up new skills and knowledge can help you shake things up and eventually move forward. But first you've got to just switch up your routine. Try getting up an hour earlier, taking on a passion project (something you've been meaning to dip into for the last few years but just haven't yet), making new friends, or setting one new goal for yourself and ditching an old one. Avoid ruminating over how long—or why—you've been in the rut. Just start taking the steps necessary to get out of it.

2. What am I really afraid of?

Career-related fears can be downright paralyzing no matter how far along you are in your professional life. When the change you're contemplating involves a financial impact, lifestyle adjustments, or what other people might think, there's a chance you're exaggerating the negative consequences and failing to act as a result.

continued

So start small. Always been interested in learning more about data analysis but haven't found the time? Find a class online or at your local community college that you can take at your own pace. Think some new photography skills might add to your portfolio as a creative professional? A nearby workshop, short-term class, or instructional session can help you get started. Once you make change a priority—and take a clear step toward it—those initial fears will start to look like speed bumps instead of towering obstacles. You'll be able to tackle unfamiliar new experiences headfirst, knowing it will just take a little effort to ramp up the learning process.

3. Do I have the right heroes?

No one's an island, as the saying goes, and it's good news for picking up new skills at any stage of your career. Mentors, coaches, bosses, and colleagues are all good candidates to help you along. Don't hesitate to reach out—or consider whether you know the right people to reach out to in the first place. If you don't, think more broadly than your existing network (but also refresh your networking efforts): Your "heroes" can include authors, athletes, entrepreneurs, inventors, or public servants—folks you might not know personally but whose ideas and instruction can help you chart a new direction.

For whatever reason, we tend to give up on the idea of "role models" after early adulthood; once you start mentoring younger people, it may feel odd to hold others up as your own "heroes." That's a mistake. Anyone you can gain insight or knowledge from—whether it's through firsthand conversation, webinars, books, or any other medium—counts as a career hero who can help you progress. Study their work, learn what makes them successful, figure out who their mentors are, and then apply those lessons in your own life.

Prying yourself out of familiarity or mediocrity isn't always easy, but it's completely doable at any age or experience level. Challenge yourself to do something new and even a little scary every day, and you'll start to feel revitalized. But it all starts with a little introspection. When things get boring or monotonous, ask yourself these three questions so you can set a new course.

—Faisal Hoque

Individual empowerment goes well beyond professional development and productivity. Individuals will also have the opportunity to approach work-life balance in a completely different context—incorporating a much more blended and interactive perspective. In particular, remote work opportunities will afford social and familial benefits that often were limited in "traditional" workplace logistics. Again, as leaders, they will have the freedom and ability to craft the sort of mix of work and play that they wish and best fits their personal and professional needs.

Regarding education, individual opportunities will cover a number of areas. As technology is increasingly incorporated into education at all levels, remote learning and other options will afford the opportunity to offer valuable education to more people. Greater access to education might also serve to mitigate the stigma of higher education only being available to the wealthy and other forms of perceived education inequality.

For these and further reasons, individual students, families, and others will enjoy growing influence in education, not only in the varied curricula available but also in how it is delivered. According to a 2021 study by Bay View Analytics titled "The Digital Learning Pulse Survey," students enrolled at colleges and universities in the United States overwhelmingly supported the continuation or increase in the use of online learning options. The majority of students, 73 percent, "somewhat" or "strongly" (46 percent) agreed that they would like to take some fully online courses in the future. A slightly smaller number of students—68 percent—indicated they would be interested in taking courses offering a combination of in-person and online instruction.[4]

The implicit message is clear. While schools at all levels scrambled to shift to online learning in response to the COVID-19 pandemic, the strengthening role of students and others as end-use consumers suggests that those changes are going to remain in place long after concern over the public health crisis has waned.

In addition, technology will make lifelong learning that much more viable and adaptable to personalization. Rather than being force-fed rote material over the first 20 years of their lives, students will be given the chance not only to continue to learn over a greater time span but also to have greater input in developing a learning program that's consistent with their interests and the needs of both themselves and society as a whole—a more fluid, flexible approach to learning.

BEST OF BOTH WORLDS

My two sons are now college-age. The older one spent two years at a junior college before COVID-19 hit, and spent his third year at a four-year university via remote learning. I was furious because I felt he needed the in-person college experience, but I also wanted him to be safe. I was mad at the world because he was being deprived (to my mind, anyway) of this amazing experience. He's actually moved up to the campus to finish his senior year now, and I'm surprised that he's admitting he prefers remote learning. I thought he would be thrilled to be around peers and live on his own for the first time in his life, but the opposite is true. He wanted to come home and attend school remotely. My husband and I were torn because of course we want to protect him, but we also wanted him to learn responsibility and grow into an adult who knows how to live independently. In the end, we basically gave him an ultimatum: Stay on campus and we would pay his tuition and board, or move home and get a job to pay for it all. It's funny how money has such an impact. He whined and fussed but ultimately chose to stay on campus. And he's actually thriving because he can mix and match classes that he attends in person or attends via Zoom. He's gotten the best of both worlds. I think had it not been for the increased global shift toward remote learning, he would have stayed at home and at junior college indefinitely.

—M. F., Librarian, Los Angeles, CA

The individual also continues to move toward the center in consumer issues. Greater access to information, buying options, marketplace feedback, and other developments have empowered consumers like never before. Not only does this afford every consumer the opportunity to make more informed purchase decisions, but consumers will also be at the forefront of new product and service development as their collective influence drives corporate strategy—a complete turnabout from a marketplace peopled with consumers who "don't know what they want until you show it to them," as Steve Jobs once remarked.[5]

But this influence isn't limited to smarter shopping and product and service development. The pandemic has also had a marked effect on individuals and how they interact with companies. The shift from individuals occupying "units" that companies could manipulate (a la Jobs' observation) has taken a 180-degree turn, as consumers drive change regarding change in corporate values. Instead of price, product quality, and other more traditional issues, an increasing number of consumers prioritize the integrity and policies of the businesses with which they associate themselves. In effect, a company's ethics and values are partially supplanting price and affordability in buying decisions.

The individual's influence in sweeping global issues such as climate change also stands to increase in the future, if for no other reason than that more people than ever have witnessed the effects of climate-related decisions firsthand. It can be surmised that the "go green" and sustainability movements are attractive to the average consumer now more than ever due in massive part to the global topic of climate change. In fact, according to a report in Forbes.com, 2020 marked a tipping point of consumer consciousness about climate change because of "escalating climate hazards" that included biblical-scale wildfires in California and floods in the Midwest that caused nearly $100 billion in damage. "Under stay-at-home orders, consumers experienced the direct link between the environment and personal well-being firsthand,"[6] the report explained. So, too, could workers and other employees accustomed to commuting learn of the drop in pollution levels as the result of working from home—further immediate, personal evidence.

A similar dynamic exists in health care. The future of health care will be centered on the consumer/patient. Twenty-four-seven access to data and information, including data regarding cost of care, will place consumers at the very heart of their health care, potentially lowering costs significantly.

HOW ARE YOU FEELING?

Experiential learning and observation can be very helpful in coming to appreciate the shift in the dynamics of health care toward the individual—often, subtle changes that can be easy to overlook. Witness the patient feedback email that often follows a visit to a health-care provider. How often did you receive that, as few as 10 years ago? It's obvious that health care at all levels is far more conscious of the overall patient experience and wants to do everything possible to ensure patient satisfaction, as well as their loyalty.

In my case, as is the situation with countless other medical organizations, my health-care provider's portal offers a direct email conduit with which I can ask my doctor questions and solicit advice and guidance. In using it for several years now, I cannot remember one instance when it took more than several hours to receive a reply—let alone my message going completely unanswered. It's these and other seemingly innocuous hints that offer meaningful evidence that the traditional physician-patient hierarchy is quickly crumbling.

—Jeff Wuorio

Likewise, a growing shift in health care, telehealth, and personal accountability for wellness has been driven by both the pandemic and the technological explosion of the Fourth Industrial Revolution. Interactive devices such as wearable health trackers are only one of many emerging such tools that are all geared to current and active patient monitoring and care.

While electronic medical records have been readily available to patients for a decade or more, health-care facilities now further engage with their patients via online portals where patients can check on their health statistics, check their diagnoses, and send messages to their caregivers without having to meet in person unless an emergency dictates it. This trend extends medical outreach to patients who are either unfit or unable to travel to their primary care physicians, as well as those who live rurally and cannot easily reach adequate medical care.

SMALL TOWN HEALTH CARE

My husband and I are originally from Los Angeles and moved to New England to semi-retire. We scouted out the area's weather, politics, and services, including health care, before we moved and were satisfied with them. Our town of 4,500 had a 75-bed hospital that's been mentioned as a top small hospital by a respected, major US news magazine. However, despite the town's small size, patients have to wait four to six weeks to get an appointment with their doctors. New patients must wait two to three months. My husband went to the local emergency room with a hot spot on his leg and was diagnosed with an infection, only to be sent home with topical cream. By the next morning, he couldn't walk without intense pain and, upon readmittance to the emergency room, recorded a white cell count of 40,000, which is a state of sepsis that could have killed him. Had it not been for a New York–based doctor traveling through the area, we're certain he wouldn't have made it. He spent nine days in the ICU with the doctor managing his care and the local doctors constantly questioning the treatment protocols at every turn. Ever since that nearly deadly incident, we have chosen to drive to Dartmouth Hitchcock Medical Center (DHMC) in New Hampshire (a three-hour

continued

round trip) for all our medical needs outside of annual checkups. We would stay in this area were it not for the shoddy health care. With DHMC, we both enjoy telehealth appointments (even pre-COVID-19) and 24/7 access to our health-care providers. Referrals are instant and follow-ups timely. This accessibility, availability, and ready interaction have been quite encouraging for us and have put us in control of better managing our medical needs.

—Shelley Moench-Kelly

One additional area of growing individual influence is the public sector. As is the case with other areas of society, governments now serve a citizenry that has unprecedented access to news, information, and data. Given the rise of a more informed community, governments will be challenged to approach these connected citizens as empowered consumers—consumers whose level of satisfaction and constructive engagement will hinge on confidence that they're receiving genuine returns on their investments in government.

Evidence of the greater role of the individual in government is already appearing in many parts of the world. For instance, at the national level, Denmark's groundbreaking MindLab was established in 2002 as one of the first government policy laboratories. The lab was tasked with developing creative, citizen-focused approaches to the ways in which policies are designed. (The lab has since been supplanted by the Disruption Task Force to further explore varied benefits of new technologies, data, and business models.)

Armed with new technology, a different mindset, and greatly enlarged expectations, the individual has and will continue to exert a growing influence across any number of the elements of daily life. But the individual isn't alone in the opportunity created by a climate of disruption and change. Business and industry are also positioned to capture enormous opportunity—exciting prospects that are by no means limited to a profit and loss statement.

CHAPTER 5—LEARN AND TRANSFORM

1. Experiential learning and close observation are critical to pinpoint just how the individual—including you—is growing in influence and authority. While examples such as health-care portals, growing application of remote and flexible work, and other instances are perhaps the most obvious and visible, keep an eye out for more beneath-the-radar signs that many dynamics of everyday life are increasingly shifting toward the individual. For instance, does your employer seem more interested in soliciting feedback from employees and taking proactive steps to help ensure that the work environment is supportive and constructive? Did a company or organization with which you dealt—which never sent a "How did we do?" sort of email—now shoot you several? Being aware of these and other seemingly minute issues can reinforce your appreciation of your growing influence, further prompting you to act upon that leverage.

2. A constant theme that has run through the exponential change and evolution the world is experiencing—particularly with regard to technology—is the issue of responsibility. As has been noted throughout this book, concern about the responsible use of new types of technology is rampant. So much so, in fact, that some manufacturers and developers have hesitated to release some products for fear that they may be misused. Additionally, legislators and other lawmakers throughout the world have called for new laws and regulations that can help guide the use of technology toward responsible, constructive applications.

That's empathy—a concern regarding the impact of actions and events on others. As the individual in varied capacities grows in influence, he or she should embrace that same level of awareness and empathy. While growing individual impact affords us all significant opportunities to drive and enact change, it's imperative that we all remain aware of the effects of that influence on those around us. Phrased another way, being put in the driver's seat is only part of individual opportunity—it's also critical that that driver make responsible, constructive decisions to avoid doing others harm, even inadvertently.

3. Individuals need to plan and act as systematically as anyone else to help them make the most of the growing opportunities afforded them. Influence unto itself is important, but it only becomes impactful if it's applied thoughtfully and with reasoned consideration. A simple but common example: The city council of a particular municipality proposes issuance of construction bonds to underwrite much-needed infrastructure improvements. Far too often, citizens' feedback and input on such issues are often confined to rambling, ill-prepared opinions at public meetings—a situation that can inevitably blow up into shouting arguments that not only cement ill feelings but can also prevent anything of constructive value getting done. A systematic approach, on the other hand, involves much more thought and potential research. First, can your opinions be best shared in a public meeting or in a letter to the editor? Has anyone considered other funding options? Additionally, how can you best share your position in a spirit of constructive empathy, focused on finding viable solutions rather than name-calling and baseless back-and-forth accusations? (Does that remind you of anyone operating on a national stage? Emulate them, and you're headed for the same pointless gridlock and maddening stalemates.)

CHAPTER 6

THE OPPORTUNITY IN BUSINESS— FINANCIAL AND ETHICAL

BUSINESSES ARE VERY MUCH LIKE individuals so far as change is concerned: If things in the past worked reasonably well, anything new can come across as unknown, untried, and unsettling. In other words, "If it ain't broke, don't fix it."

That may be so, but the reality is that the drivers of change are opening up significant new opportunities for businesses of all sorts—opportunities that are not necessarily focused exclusively on the bottom line and with potentially greater import than any profit and loss statement.

One of the most significant points of opportunity has to do with the simple logistics of work and business. The COVID-19 pandemic has not only changed the way human beings interact with each other but also reinvented the way companies and businesses operate—internally, as well as how they present themselves to their customer base and the public at large.

As detailed in the prior chapter, the global effect of the pandemic initially laid waste to companies' traditional work structures for its employees. Prior to COVID-19, remote work was a privilege enjoyed mostly by executives and freelancers. Because of the pandemic, however, masses of workers who formerly held desk jobs at a corporate headquarters now work from their living and dining rooms—a more mainstream and pervasive reality than ever before.

The benefits of expanded remote and flexible work arrangements for the individual were addressed in chapter 5, among them greater productivity and employee satisfaction. But businesses also stand to enjoy a varied array of positive outcomes that, to a certain extent, have had to be force-fed upon them.

One such example lies in lowered business expenses. Be it through need for less office space, equipment, travel expenses, and other associated operating costs, businesses are poised to pocket significant savings by decreases in the protocols and necessities of what was formerly "business as usual." In fact, one company can save more than $10,000 for each remote worker who telecommutes to work 50 percent of the time, according to Global Workplace Analytics Telework Savings Calculator.[1] Obviously enough, those saved funds could go elsewhere, from increased employee benefits to expanded public outreach, which, as will be examined, is becoming critical amid shifting consumer interests and priorities.

Another plus is increased access to applicants, particularly well-qualified ones. A company that is open to remote work arrangements not only may boost the number of applicants it can consider—since location is now less of a consideration—but also stands to attract applicants for whom remote work arrangements is an enticing, if not somewhat mandatory, benefit. As we write this, businesses of all sorts are challenged to find employees, let alone topflight talent. A capacity to come into contact with a larger range of applicants who may be able to work in some sort of alternative arrangement could be a competitive boon to recruiting efforts.

Fig. 6.1. Photo by Jonathan Francisca on Unsplash.

Moreover, a less centralized work arrangement can also prove exceedingly beneficial during emergencies, such as natural disasters. While something such as a hurricane or tornado could completely cripple a business whose workers are located in a common setting, remote workers may be able to carry on with their responsibilities even if other parts of the operation have been shut down. An added plus is that such a network is already in place, resulting in less "scrambling" to piece together work arrangements and less time spent by employees coming up to speed with what is already familiar technology.

That may be particularly important, given climate change's impact on more frequent and devastating natural events, from flooding to wildfires. Adoption of comprehensive remote work networks can prove an effective, proactive step in dealing with the possibility of such occurrences, not to mention add greater impetus to business's role in central climate change issues.

AN EARTHQUAKE'S "DAMAGE"

I worked in Los Angeles at the time of the 1994 Northridge earthquake. It measured 6.7 on the Richter scale, and all 200 employees at our headquarters had no way of contacting one another, much less upper management. We all showed up to work as normal, only to find the building standing but looking as if a bomb exploded. Each floor had four-by-eight-foot windows offering 360-degree views that now lay shattered on the grass at ground level. Green bar reports—old-school green-and-white spooled paper used in dot-matrix printers—from the offices closest to those windows lay strewn across the manicured walkways that circled the three-story building, as did personal effects, including plants, personal framed photos and desk ephemera, stuffed animals, rubber band balls, and the like. Operations were shut down completely for one week as city engineers evaluated the building's safety. All the windows were boarded up for three months afterward as replacement windows were fabricated.

Not only did the quake's impact directly affect our work for one week, but the longer-lasting effects of PTSD showed up pretty quickly as well. In an environment that used to be open with amazing views of the city, workers felt as if they were trapped in underground, bombed-out shelters. We had greater numbers of employees calling in sick and taking more frequent smoke breaks. Our manager was so traumatized that she walked out after the second day back, never to return or speak to any of us again. The vending machines had to be restocked twice as often as before the quake, and on-site crisis counselors were employed. Staff (ours and company-wide) constantly called in sick for the next six months, and we knew those sick days weren't due to colds or the flu. When concerned coworkers asked for details, many of the employees calling in would respond with vague answers, mostly putting the "blame" on a sick child or older relative. No one wanted to be outed as needing counseling or mental time off. It was taboo back in those days and never spoken of. I think back to that time and know that had we had the opportunity to work remotely so we all could heal in the safety of our own homes, the negative effects surely would have been lessened.

—Shelley Moench-Kelly

Still another plus for businesses is the experience and training that more autonomous work arrangements can provide. Workers who are now self-managing to a larger extent are almost certainly acquiring greater and more varied skill sets, such as time management, decision-making, and other positive abilities. While those may not necessarily have an immediate impact on operations and profitability, over a longer time frame a more "complete" employee stands to contribute more to the organization for which he or she works. Developing additional skills and leadership attributes can prompt greater upward in-house movement by employees, which can also foster greater employee retention, particularly in an employment environment where employees and job seekers are enjoying increasing overall leverage. The more current employees have an opportunity to grow and evolve, the more they will tend to keep those improved skills in-house.

However appealing remote work can be on any number of levels, implementation of any sort of flexible work arrangement need not happen as quickly and haphazardly as it had to amid COVID-19—nor should it. It's important for businesses to systemically develop and present a culture that not only showcases commitment to remote work arrangements but also details the philosophy and guidelines that underscore a flexible work program. First, to attract top talent for remote employment, it's important that a business or organization's digital presence is every bit as top of the line. Remote work applicants situated far away from a business have only websites and other online features with which to gauge a company. A shoddy website or an inoperable one can send the wrong message to would-be employees.

FIRST IMPRESSIONS

As someone who has worked remotely for decades, I can attest to the value of an impressive online and digital presence. As many would-be clients are located far from my physical location, that's

continued

often all I have to judge them on professionalism, values, and commitment to the people with whom they work. I have seen websites for organizations that would have otherwise attracted my interest, save for a shoddy, almost plug-and-play-like website. The same can be said for websites that are simply too complicated, are too difficult to maneuver in, or simply come across as too flashy.

It's best to keep digital identity polished, straightforward, and welcoming. Anything that deviates too far from that can seem cheap and irresponsible or, in the case of too many bells and whistles, can make visitors wonder why the message needs so much embellishment. In the evolving world of remote and flexible work, a solid website is the first step to attracting and keeping interest from talented would-be employees.

—Jeff Wuorio

Further, make sure that comprehensive policies are in place governing remote work. That may seem obvious, but companies relatively new to remote work arrangements can often assume that flex work is just the same as in-person employment, just in a different setting. That could be true to a certain extent, but issues such as work hours, scheduling, check-ins with supervisors, reimbursement for expenses, and other protocols should be addressed and reviewed to make certain that remote workers understand what's acceptable and what is not—and, for management, what must be adjusted to accommodate remote work.

The increasing use of remote workers also affords businesses the unique opportunity for crisis planning. As noted earlier, in times of natural disaster or some other similar event, remote workers can help keep things operating as normally as possible. To leverage that to the utmost, companies should devote significant time and energy to developing a thoughtful, comprehensive emergency work plan, including which remote workers are equipped with certain tools, the hierarchy of command during emergency situations, and other protocols and policies so that remote work systems can continue to operate as effectively as possible.

Shelley's story about the earthquake and its aftermath also underscores an additional opportunity for businesses of all types. As noted previously, work-from-home arrangements can also dovetail into policies and procedures that address an employee's entire well-being, including emotional and psychological. Taking that commitment and applying it to all employees, on-site and otherwise, affords business leadership a unique chance at broad-based empathy—to make all workers happier and healthier, not to mention more candid about those sorts of personal needs. Employees should never again have to disguise the real reason for "calling in sick" or for slogging on needlessly at work when it's obvious they have crippling issues with which they're trying to deal.

The peripheral issue of combatting climate change is another point of opportunity for business and industry, albeit in something of a convoluted manner. As has been addressed, on the surface, greater availability of remote work arrangements has reduced industry's carbon footprint. For instance, pollution rates in China dropped by nearly 11 percent in the first half of 2020.[2] Given many workers' enthusiastic embrace of remote and flexible work arrangements, estimates hold that the United States could reduce the amount of greenhouse gasses permeating the atmosphere by tens of millions through broad-based acceptance of alternative work arrangements.

An additional aspect of opportunity for businesses of all sizes is the message such efforts to trim pollution sends to consumers. Given individual consumers' growing prioritization of a company's green persona, doing right by the climate affords businesses a readily available means to portray themselves as climate-aware, proactive citizens. That has been shown to boost consumer appeal considerably in terms of buying decisions and loyalty—a critical element of client empathy and awareness of customers' mindsets and priorities.

In fact, that appeal is rather overwhelming. According to a survey of more than 1,000 consumers in the United States and the United Kingdom, 96 percent of people feel their own actions, such as donating, recycling, or buying ethically, can make a difference to the environment, with half characterizing that as a significant difference. That staggering percentage also includes consumers' interest in buying from companies that display ecology awareness, even down to the use of recyclable shipping labels and packaging.[3] Even in such seemingly innocuous actions as buying simple items, consumers' priorities are focused on green—even companies without an overt connection to the environment will do well by identifying this dynamic.

But whether business fully leverages the opportunity inherent in ecological positioning remains to be seen. First and foremost, how long any benefit from reduced carbon emissions lasts depends to a large extent on the level and length of commitment on the part of businesses to continue to maintain remote work arrangements after they're no longer medically necessary. For instance, a company that uses remote workers during the COVID-19 pandemic will hardly be seen as ecologically aware should it require all employees to return to on-site jobs when such a significant shift seems unnecessary, if not utterly counterproductive.

Further, the actual benefits of reduced on-site employee work can be compromised by other factors. On the one hand, many businesses, such as Microsoft, Facebook, and Google, have pledged to become carbon neutral by 2050.[4] Others, including Twitter, have publicly announced plans to make remote work available whenever possible.

The issue is that those pledges to reduce carbon emissions and other forms of pollution, however admirable, apply exclusively to companies' on-site facilities—not necessarily to employees' homes. There, suggest some researchers, emissions from food and power sources still exist, and quite possibly at levels that more than offset what is being reduced at a company work site. In effect, left unchanged, everyday home habits and activities can be as environmentally destructive as commuting cars and packed office facilities.

Additionally, less ongoing time spent face-to-face may lead to more frequent, involved travel, such as increased airplane travel. Since five flights a year for 2,000 employees can produce thousands of tons of CO_2 emissions, cutting pollution by keeping the car in the garage may be largely mitigated by more ecologically damaging forms of travel.

How businesses handle these delicate issues related to remote work will dictate the amount of opportunity that can be realized, both financially and socially. With regard to travel, as the pandemic begins to loosen its grip on both business and society in general, some companies have proactively announced plans to trim travel. In particular, intracompany meetings, training, and other like activities will increasingly be handled via Zoom, with travel budgets focused more specifically on trips to meet with clients, prospects, and other meetings where personal contact is more important.

Additionally, not only will businesses be charged with carefully weighing their overall environmental impact beyond any decision to simply incorporate remote work, but they should also consider educational efforts geared to remote workers on the essentials of reducing carbon impact, no matter where they happen to work most of the time. That could help offset any increases in home-generated pollution. One possible strategy would be to emulate workplace procedures and habits at home, such as printing paper on both sides, using energy-efficient lighting, and other steps. Again, such an effort to make its environmental impact as meaningful and long lasting as possible could attract clients and customers for whom such values are an essential shopping point—not to mention be a potentially competitive advantage from a public relations standpoint over companies that approach the environment with lower levels of energy and commitment.

As touched on earlier, another dicey issue having to do with remote work is as much a public relations matter as it is a practical one. Many

THE WORKING PARENT

My daughter is two years old, and my husband's hours were cut by 25 percent due to the pandemic. I needed to get a job to support his salary that also allowed me to work from home because we can't afford a babysitter or day care. I found a job as a virtual assistant to an executive, and I love it. I'm challenged enough to keep myself sharp, but not so stressed that I take it out on my family. My boss has children of her own and gives me complete freedom to tend to my daughter whenever I need, as long as I get my work done. My husband and I never would have imagined this scenario where we both worked but were still able to spend quality time with our daughter. I hope we can continue this for a very long time. It sure beats having to commute back and forth and miss out on her growing up.

—J. S., Virtual Assistant, Long Island, NY

companies that adopted extensive remote work programs during the pandemic now hope to recall employees back to on-site employment. While that may be pragmatically valid, it can nonetheless attract criticism due to what might be viewed as a purely mercenary decision to go remote only when it was absolutely necessary—particularly so if employees were enthusiastic about flexible work arrangements and wish to retain them to some degree.

Although there are some instances where a 100 percent on-site workforce might be genuinely necessary, companies that are empathetic toward employees who enjoyed remote work might best navigate the situation by offering hybrid opportunities—half time on-site, half time elsewhere. And, if on-site is truly optimal, companies can—and are— sweetening the shift back to the office with perks, contests, and cash prizes for those employees willing to return to a physical office.

Some companies have already announced aggressive plans to reduce their carbon footprints beyond the issue of work location of employees. One such example is IKEA. The furniture manufacturer has pledged to become climate positive by 2030 through steps ranging from shifts to 100 percent renewable energy to in-house design of products with a focus on sustainability, including recycling and remanufacturing.[5]

Fig. 6.2. Photo by Samson on Unsplash.

Another example is a new company called Outlery. With more than 40,000 global backers to its overwhelmingly successful 2019 Kickstarter campaign that raised $1.2 million in two months, the company's mission to save the planet by helping to eliminate single-use plastic utensils has proven successful beyond its founder's dreams.[6] The fork, spork, knife, spoon, and chopsticks are all crafted of high-quality stainless steel and can be disassembled and stored in an aluminum tin no larger than an Altoids mints box.

Social opportunities also exist beyond the scope of climate issues. Driven by issues such as pervasive misinformation, racial tensions, and other societal issues, businesses have the opportunity to leverage overall social responsibility as a viable, pragmatic strategy. Ethical awareness, rather than just being a cosmetic option, is becoming both a necessity and a chance for businesses to connect that much more solidly with the marketplace.

With regard to misinformation, business's opportunity to help in the fight against dissemination of fake news carries more than the ethical high ground. As any business can attest, the spread of bad news, whether legitimate or not, can be devastating. Accordingly, business has a financial stake in combatting misinformation that's every bit as compelling as the moral component.

That calls for a multipronged approach. First, effective monitoring systems leveraging artificial and human intelligence can identify harmful disinformation before it has the opportunity to spread. Additionally, closer partnerships with government and other stakeholders to share patterns and significant insights more closely could better pool resources and make the overall effort to control misinformation more effective. Increased use of artificial intelligence can help in arranging and analyzing this larger amount of data to boost efforts to identify and mitigate misinformation.

Closely tied to business's social message is the development of a culture of "good work," where workers understand the ultimate impact of their work on the world around them—an opportunity that reflects changes in employee attitudes and priorities. Companies have the chance to broaden how professional "success" is defined to create ethical, aesthetic, and social value in addition to economic and material worth.

BUILDING FUTURISTS

Here are four questions to turn everyone in your company into a futurist. If you keep asking the right questions, you'll be wrong about the future less often than your competitors.

Remember what 1997 was like? How well?

It was Amazon's first full fiscal year. Microsoft's Windows 97 operating system wasn't there quite yet, and it soon became Windows 98. The internet bubble was on its way, but we couldn't see it. "Y2K" was around the corner, too, but few of us were worried yet. Google? Not for another two years. Many companies were still asking themselves if they really needed a web page, and professionals were deciding whether or not to get an email address.[7]

Most of us aren't futurists, and futurists aren't oracles.

Back then, the world of 2007 was a long way off and hard to envision, and 2017 was virtually a complete abstraction. That wasn't an abject failure on the part of the business world, of course; the future really is hard to foresee. In retrospect, however, there are always real costs to imperfect forecasting (the financial crisis being one of them, growing cybersecurity threats another) that still have to be reckoned with long afterward.

Most of us aren't futurists, and futurists aren't oracles. They simply try and make some sense of what's coming—not hard-and-fast predictions, just possibilities. The most accurate forecasts we're able to make are often necessarily broad. What's always clear is simply that technology will only burrow deeper into our world and organizations, disrupting the way we do things and throwing more threats and opportunities in our way. *How* it will is more of an open question by comparison.

Still, there are a few ways companies can get better at predicting not just what changes may be around the corner but also how they'll affect them once those disruptions arrive. Making everyone in your company more effective futurists all starts with asking the right questions. Here are a few of them.

1. What's our process for assessing the future?

Your company may not have a formal, codified method for making predictions about the future, but it definitely has a business strategy. And business strategies arise from some set of assumptions about what changes are afoot—accurate or otherwise.

That means that, functionally anyway, your company *already* makes guesses about the future all the time. What matters is the basis upon which it does, and determining that takes a little self-examination. Start by taking these steps:

continued

- Closely examine your current strategy, right here in the present. How well is your team executing your current plan? What changes are needed today? Consider those execution methods from the perspective of your immediate situation to determine whether changing circumstances are likely to make your organization more or less effective.

- Analyze the impact of the current work of your team, partners, and customers. Where are the most obvious places your results can be improved or revenue increased?

- Evaluate your present capabilities for making those improvements. What assets and resources do you have at your command to try something new?

If this type of assessment sounds a little too present-focused, don't worry. The assumptions you're making about the future are embedded directly in the way you're doing things right now. Most people inside organizations—frontline workers all the way on up to execs—don't often take time to think through them. Closely reexamining your existing processes can make it easier to see the type of future that your current strategy assumes you're heading toward.

2. How are we reading the news?

For many of us, innovations in the tech sector tend to be harbingers of change everywhere. Many business leaders' predictions hinge on an aggregated, subjective sense of what they read in the news. And that's not a bad place to start. But it's the inferences we can make about the cutting-edge innovations that truly matter, and making more studied extrapolations takes practice.

Let's take just one example from a 2016 article from Vice.com titled "The Internet of Things Is Just a Pit Stop on the Way to Smart Dust." It refers to an Internet of Things (IoT) technology that's based on tiny sensors that can be scattered around, then report back to a network on the environment—noise, light, chemicals, vibration, temperature, and the like. And on the horizon are radio-frequency identification tags the size of pinheads that could be attached to any product as it makes its way through manufacturing and distribution.

As information becomes more plentiful and less centralized, more organizations are likely to decentralize too.

If you work in accounting or for a chemical company, for instance, "smart dust" may seem little more than a sci-fi curiosity, especially since IoT as a whole seems to have hit some serious obstacles lately.

But while the specifics may not directly impact you or your industry, the underlying trend of such an innovation certainly does. What it hints is that we'll be inundated by a new wave of information as the planet becomes increasingly connected. These are some baseline inferences we can make about how that wave will unfurl, even if individual technologies have wildly different fates:

- Anything that can be digitized will be.

- Anything that can go wireless will.

- Anything that can get smaller will.

- And information will want to move more freely.

These technological transformations will continue to reshape the way the business world is organized. As information becomes more plentiful and less centralized, more organizations are likely to decentralize too in order to respond swiftly to it all.

In keeping track of news developments, don't get overwhelmed by the details, but don't disregard them either. Just think analysis first and synthesis second: That big new merger that's getting so much buzz—what does it reveal about the buyer's priorities and instincts about what's coming? Or that new technology that's still years away from hitting the market, the one you keep hearing about in dribs and drabs—what preceding tech is it building upon or threatening to eventually supplant?

Then start connecting those dots: Are other companies all making similar bets? Is there another existing technology whose fate might be sealed by that sci-fi-sounding one? Developing this kind of integrated sense of the changes you're hearing about—however disparately—can help you sharpen your futurist muscles. Just making some time in company meetings (even 15 minutes a week) to talk through some of the latest business and tech news together can bring that habit to your entire team.

continued

3. Are we constantly testing what we think is working fine?

When business and technology aren't integrated, all sorts of bad things can happen. The most common culprit for this lack of integration is untested assumptions about the relationship between the two.

For instance, software designed to automate an existing business process may only speed up an inefficient or ineffective process that isn't contributing maximum business value–even though you assume that Technology X is automating Process Y. "We have something in place that's already doing that," you may imagine. But can you confirm it's actually working?

It can cut the other way, too. Adapting processes to fit the rules embedded in software may eliminate some activity that differentiates the company and gives it an advantage—at least temporarily, until what you assume about the competition is no longer true. In both of these cases, the outside world is changing more rapidly than ever; this sometimes presents a change before a project is implemented.

Sometimes end users change their minds. Sometimes they balk at anything new that is imposed on them. Sometimes techies fall in love with new technology for its own sake. Sometimes they are never asked what new technology is available that might improve a business process. Little wonder that so many technology projects fail! The only way around this is to constantly test the basic beliefs that undergird your company's choices—to know as soon as possible when certain "solutions" (technological or otherwise) are no longer actually solving anything, even if they once did.

But the answer here isn't to try and turn over every single stone again and again. It's to keep asking, "What is our purpose?" In other words, why are you here, and what purpose does your company serve? And are you serving that purpose as effectively this month as you were last month? If not, how come? And the answer to *that* will lead you to those broken links in your organization as soon as they break.

4. How are we managing information?

Imagine for a moment the building you work in is stripped of its walls to reveal the plumbing infrastructure—pipes bringing water into the building and distributing it. Imagine now the various uses to which it's put: someone washing their hands with hot water on one floor, someone else using cold on another, a water heater providing hot water, a water fountain cooling it, and so on.

Now imagine the building's information infrastructure—telephone and internet wiring, boxes for incoming and outgoing snail mail, cable television connections, wireless routers, and so on—taking information from the outside or inside and distributing it.

Then picture the users of this information. An executive studies a computer dashboard of operational data, an employee surfs the web, an administrative assistant sifts through the paper mail, a committee meets and hears a report, email flows endlessly, operational plans are printed and bound and put on a shelf, and on and on.

New ideas float along these "flows" of information. And a leader's task is twofold: Ensure that you have the right flows in place, and create "filters" that capture the most valuable ideas while discarding the stuff that isn't useful or relevant.

How do you set up those filters? In general, information can be managed in three ways. One is through organizational structures, such as decision-making groups. Another is in processes—who hands off what information to whom. The other is through automation—technology that gathers and presents data, such as customer relationship management data from a website.

But while it's vital to view your organization as an information collector, processor, and distributor all at once, it's just as important to see and act upon something *new* in all that information. The futurist Amy Webb outlines a handful of questions on how to spot fake trends on FastCompany.com that anybody can ask themselves in order to distinguish a genuine trend from something that's merely "trending"—to tell the proverbial signal from the noise. To paraphrase three of her criteria (although there's more than that)—

- A trend is timely but persists over time.
- A trend evolves even while it's still emerging.
- The dots connect more and more as the trend goes mainstream.

continued

We can't predict the future. But we can make sure the next generation of leaders is prepared to live it, make sense of it, and orchestrate its upheavals as strategically as possible. That takes learning, experimentation, and a little bit of luck.

But it also just takes practice. And as long as you can get everyone inside your organization to keep asking the right questions, you're likely to be wrong about the future less often than your competitors are.

—Faisal Hoque

Even though a fully remote workforce remains practically impossible for a number of businesses and industries whose operations mandate on-site work activity, businesses and those employees who have to continue to show up in person stand to benefit from greatly improved worker safety systems and protocols. Analysts at the London-based Social Market Foundation explain further that the use of robotics and connected devices "has significant potential to make the workplace safer" and that robots will, with increased frequency, undertake relatively dangerous tasks, such as lifting and moving heavy objects. The firm also points out that AI, data analytics, and connected devices could help improve workers' mental health at work by checking if employees are working excessive hours or not taking their lunch breaks.[8]

The technological innovations and advances already appearing as a result of the Fourth Industrial Revolution (4IR) also stand to offer business and industry enormous opportunity in what can be seen as a major shift in core function and activity. Although, according to the London-based *Training Journal,* potentially millions of jobs could be disrupted because of automation from 4IR: "The automation of standard tasks will generate huge productivity gains, which could add billions of pounds to the UK economy. New jobs and new companies will be created, and they could bring richer, more rewarding and engaging roles, oriented around creativity and human relationships, rather than the execution of repetitive tasks."[9] Phrased another way—if the robots do, indeed, come and "take over" many of our traditional jobs, they stand to replace them with more sophisticated, rewarding, and better-paid opportunities. That's great news for employees looking to break out of workplace ruts and businesses hoping to attract new talent with appealing, more sophisticated work. It's also a great opportunity for businesses to attract and retain topflight talent.

The exponentially growing drive for work that's both satisfying and lucrative has also taken other avenues. After years of sliding entrepreneurial activity, remarkably enough, more than four million new businesses were started in 2020, according to a study by the DC-based Peterson Institute for International Economics.[10] Even employees and workers uninterested in going out on their own are taking it upon themselves to prepare for a radically different work environment—38 percent of workers pursued additional training in 2020, compared with only 14 percent in the prior year, says a study by Udemy, a workplace education concern.[11] Businesses have the opportunity to fully leverage these sorts of better-trained employees if they can develop forward-thinking programs and work opportunities that are positioned to use these types of advanced skills and abilities.

With the introduction of new technology, many businesses and industries are identifying completely new ways of serving existing needs and markets. That's particularly true with agile, innovative companies that, with access to global digital platforms for research, development, marketing, sales, and distribution, can improve the quality, speed, or price at which value is delivered.

Customer service is one such area that is poised to reinvent itself. Rather than supplanting human customer service representatives and other support personnel, 4IR's technology infusion will allow for greater efficiency and performance, as well as a wider range of consumer options.

Training is an ideal example. Traditionally a one-size-fits-all arrangement, technology such as sentiment analysis tools—software that analyzes text conversations and evaluates the tone, intent, and emotion inherent in spoken words—will make it easier to identify each customer service rep's strengths and weaknesses, allowing more personalized training to better each employee's performance. Employees who need to sharpen their technical skills will be able to do so, as will tech-savvy workers who need to improve softer, more interpersonal skills.

The increased presence of data in all its varied forms is yet another stark opportunity for business. Foreshadowing this trend, British data scientist Clive Humby coined the phrase "data is the new oil" in 2006[12]—today and in the future, that means the key to surviving and thriving is harnessing as much data as possible and maximizing its usage to remain competitive. According to the *EU Business News*, during the period from 2010 to 2018, global patent filings for smart connected objects rose by an average annual rate of 20 percent—"most notable in the areas of connectivity and data management."[13] Clearly, business notices the enormous opportunity in a tsunami of information and data that needs to be handled and used in the most effective manner possible.

More opportunities for business growth, impact, and empowerment can be created through data collection, data sharing, and creative collaborations so entities can better connect with the marketplace, address consumer preferences, and save money on travel and hardware costs. This powerful trend preceded many current powerful disrupters, such as the COVID-19 pandemic, and shows no sign of slowing down. For instance, in the last decades leading up to Y2K, American fast-food chains such as Taco Bell, Kentucky Fried Chicken (KFC), Carl's Jr., and Green Burrito existed as single, standalone entities. In the early 2000s, blended locations began popping up around Southern California, starting with Taco Bell and KFC teaming up, then Carl's Jr. partnering with Green Burrito. For couples or families who couldn't decide where to eat, this unique setup was the perfect combination and certainly a by-product of extensive data collection and analysis supporting this more hybrid approach to dining.

Business education programs are already responding to the need for top-tier data handling and analysis skills. For instance, DC-based Georgetown University has launched two new specialized degree programs—one a master's degree in management that focuses on technology and innovation, and an MS in business analytics that prepares leaders to understand and use data to make value-based decisions. The university is also focusing research on understanding how to use algorithms in decision-making, the need for updated telecommunication and trade policies, and how robo-advisors can help individuals make better financial decisions.

Schools are also taking the point with regard to training business leaders in collaborative and complementary methodology. For example, Georgetown has also introduced its first joint undergraduate degree incorporating a BS in business and global affairs with Georgetown's School of Foreign Service. This program focuses on new ways to understand the intersection of business issues, public policy, and diplomacy.

Change is also having an internal impact on business in other ways. The shifting nature of work itself will afford organizations the opportunity to learn about and embrace teamwork as a genuine organizational entity, rather than cheerleading or an exercise in habit. One example of this is a new work philosophy called "We Working." This involves designing small and flexible teams in response to fluctuating workloads, shrinking time frames, and intense flurries of information exchange and coordination. We Working encourages businesses to create small, autonomous, high-performing teams that form, converge, act, and dismantle as assignments change. Fueled by autonomy and shared trust, We Working reduces the need for human managers to assemble teams and monitor performance.

Overall, business and industry have the opportunity to serve as examples of the sort of comprehensive and genuine change that's possible during a time of enormous disruption. The business world has the power and influence to truly dive into systemic causes for racism, gender inequality, and bias and to take both internal and external steps to address them.

Internally, that can mean actionable policies to increase diversity. Publicly, companies are putting their money where their mouths are with regard to focused philanthropic giving, such as YouTube's $1 million pledge to the Center for Policing Equity, and Glossier's donation of $500,000 to support racial justice organizations and another $500,000 to Black-owned beauty brands.[14] Again, businesses that maintain that kind of level of support for social causes and movements over a long period of time will stand to benefit most from positive consumer response.

CHAPTER 6—LEARN AND TRANSFORM

1. A primary opportunity driven by exponential change is the expansion of customer and marketplace appeal beyond issues such as price. Companies that practice an active form of empathy to maintain close contact with their customers' priorities are recognizing that factors such as social responsibility, environmental practices, employee relations, and other issues are playing a growing role in consumer decision-making. However companies maintain that contact—by way of blogs, consumer feedback opportunities, surveys, and other means—will prove essential to staying in step with the shifting values of their markets. And as change continues to take hold and evolve, technologically and otherwise, the more critical that commitment to empathy will become.

2. The war against misinformation is one such area of opportunity that's of particular importance to the business community—in more ways than one. For one thing, systemically planned and executed partnerships with government and other businesses and organizations can boost all efforts to identify and mitigate misinformation through the power of shared resources. Not only do such social

commitments serve as a powerful marketing tool to consumers, but it's also smart business, as misinformation, left unchecked, can be destructive to businesses of all sorts by spreading falsehoods and other "news" that can harm both reputations and bottom lines.

3. Businesses of all sorts also need to keep reminding themselves that this, for better or worse, is a brand-new world in many ways where many so-called rules and realities have yet to be firmly established. Accordingly, a mindset that emphasizes and is comfortable with experiential learning is valuable, not merely to identify new opportunities but also to start to learn what sorts of strategies and ideas will prove effective in a constantly evolving environment. The textbook of opportunity has yet to be written in full, so a focus on experiential and ongoing learning will prove critical to navigating change successfully.

CHAPTER 7

THE OPPORTUNITY IN EDUCATION—THE "FLIPPED CLASSROOM"

LIKE OTHER AREAS DISRUPTED by change on various fronts, education at all levels is facing a greatly empowered consumer. That shift in influence affords education a variety of opportunities to change, adapt, and, perhaps most important, turn away from many philosophic and systemic practices that many consider completely broken and outdated—if not simply destructive.

On a global level, education has the opportunity to recraft what education genuinely means. Going back for countless generations, education has had an inherent emphasis on "training"—imbuing students with sufficient skills to become productive members of the workforce and little else. Even after the ultimate destinations for many of these students—for instance, factories and mills—largely disappeared, education has yet to completely pivot away from the goal of molding young people with sufficient basic skills and education to perform rudimentary work tasks.

If nothing else, that clearly mandates a shift away from traditional learning to more sophisticated material and methodology that will equip students to work effectively with the varied new forms of technology they will inevitably encounter. That lies, in part, in needed improvements to elements of STEM curricula (science, technology, engineering, and math), in addition to other adaptations and revisions in other areas of learning.

But the necessity for more advanced and pertinent skills also highlights another area where education has the opportunity to adapt for the better. Given the complexity, sophistication, and import of much of the new technology produced from the Fourth Industrial Revolution, education will also be charged with teaching students the values and beliefs with which such technology can be used both effectively and morally. In so doing, education can help address the widespread concern of powerful technology being exploited irresponsibly and unethically.

Teaching about the morality of technology may seem almost cosmetic to some, but it's far more substantial in its impact. First is the practical. Ignoring the right and wrong of powerful new technology is akin to teaching a teenager to drive without paying attention to any road signs and warnings. Moreover, in failing to leverage this opportunity, educational systems at all levels will help fuel fear of technology being used to violate privacy and supplant human labor rather than connect and serve.

That effort needs to begin early in students' lives and progress exponentially. Rather than suggesting that technology is something that users have to be very careful with, education should emphasize that technology is another means through which students can express their personal values and ethics. Teachers can leverage online curricula from organizations such as iLearn, BlogSafety, NetFamilyNews, and Responsible Netizen to ingrain responsible behavior and practices at an early age rather than having to "correct" bad habits later in life.

A related opportunity lies in the development of other somewhat softer skills, such as creativity, critical thinking, collaboration, empathy, and other similar attributes. Although technology at its highest form can perform certain tasks better than humans, people using that technology will need to be equipped with mindsets and ways of thinking that complement technology's advantages. That will further people's ability to partner with and leverage technology rather than feeling as though they're somehow "competing" with the machines—perhaps in a struggle, real or imagined, to save their jobs and livelihoods.

Fig. 7.1. Photo by Charlotte May from Pexels.

This critical need for education and training with a different focus has already attracted the attention of business leaders and executives. According to the World Economic Forum's "The Future of Jobs 2018," executives expressed a strong preference for employees with critical-thinking and collaboration skills over those with top-notch technical abilities.[1]

SOFT SKILLS MATTER

The ability to think critically is closely aligned with the application of mindfulness. In my previous book *Everything Connects*, I explained the concept of mindfulness, of being and living in the moment. Expanding on this as it relates to the Fourth Industrial Revolution and opportunities for education lies in the development of "soft skills" in addition to the technical, business, and other "hard skills" that most companies and schools foster. Soft skills (i.e., "people skills") include emotional intelligence, empathy, confidence, and integrity.[2] In this era of technology and automation—where news articles foreshadow a time when robots will take over our jobs, technology vendors churn out new innovations on an almost-daily basis, and companies scramble to find alternative sources of labor—where do the humanities stand? In my view, the skills that come from a strong education in the humanities are becoming more important than ever.[3]

Here are some tips to awaken and nurture your own soft skills.[4]

1. **Capitalize on your strengths.** Focus on understanding your strengths (such as strategic thinking, influencing, or relationship building), and then leverage them to your advantage instead of fixating on your weaknesses.

2. **Break out of your shell once in a while.** For example, if the thought of speaking to a group sends shivers down your spine, join a local Toastmasters group. If you aren't used to working on a team, get involved with some volunteer groups,

and start working for some good causes. And if your communication skills could use a good polish, join an improv class. The more experiential the learning, the more valuable the learning experience. You're doing, not just hearing about or reading.

3. **Don't be afraid to go against the grain.** High schools and universities may be pushing STEM educations, but that doesn't mean everyone needs a technical background to have a successful career. A recent study of 1,700 people from 30 countries found that the majority of those in leadership positions had either a social sciences or humanities degree. It works in all sorts of professional and academic applicants. According to Medical School Admission Requirements, more than half of all philosophy students who applied to medical school in one year were accepted—perhaps as "un-science-y" a field of study as you can imagine. By contrast, less than 40 percent of all applicants who were biology majors won acceptance to med school.[5] The message—we want people who know how to think. Medical training can always come later.

4. **Modify, reuse, and automate to your advantage.** For example, as an author, I first write small blog posts, the posts turn into full-length articles, and articles become the basis of a new book. Reusing gives us speed and efficiency without reinventing the wheel every time we want to create a new asset.

5. **Practice mindfulness by staying focused on one task at a time.** If we have too much information inundating us at the same time, our brain cannot differentiate between what is important and what isn't, negatively affecting our memory. When we remain focused on one task at a time—meaning we are being mindful of the present—we find the results to be a greater success than if we were to attempt to multitask.

—Faisal Hoque

In effect, education at all levels has the very real opportunity to help craft citizens of value to society. As education no longer needs to focus so exclusively on career readiness, education can help shape values and create a place where students can develop a vision for the world that *they* want to create. That's a much broader view of the value of education than has been traditionally embraced.

The growing hunger for "good work" also plays a role in this significant shift. With students increasingly seeking to understand the ultimate impact of their work on the world around them, going to school to get a job could be replaced with—or, at the very least, augmented by—critical learning that emphasizes practical decision-making, problem-solving, and collaboration. As a result, schools at all levels can respond with programs geared to these sorts of soft skills.

VOLUNTARY CURIOSITY

The issue of softer skills and diversified learning raises a potentially dicey question. When I was in college many years ago, "distribution requirements" were often the bane of our existence. A biology major suffering through a class on modern American literature could empathize with the English major drowsing through geology. Granted, even then we all tried to appreciate that such academic mandates were supposed to make us well-rounded citizens who were comfortable outside our area of "expertise" and interest. Whether that happened or not is another question, but, nonetheless, required classes to graduate seemed to have good intentions.

Now that we're careening into an era of greater student input and perhaps an even greater emphasis on broad-based learning, what becomes of these sorts of academic must-dos? On the one hand, many in the academic world are urging colleges and universities to drop the practice of graduation requirements, claiming they're outdated and ineffective. On the other hand, if education is becoming increasingly more self-directed, what assurance is there that students will voluntarily step outside their comfort zone? If, by chance, distribution and other types of requirements are eliminated, schools and educators will be charged with building interest in students to delve into topics unrelated to their primary interests without a prescribed mandate. If they can pull it off, students will benefit from a broader, more diverse academic environment without the feeling of being forced to—a win-win in today's changing educational goals and priorities.

—Jeff Wuorio

These and other shifts in the nature and objectives of education will also afford the opportunity to broaden students' perspectives. Just as technology and other tools have served to bring the world closer together, education can help students develop a greater sense of international awareness of the synergy and systems that connect everyone. Not only will this recasting of mindsets prove essential to working effectively with greater technological connectivity, but it may also help combat the pervasive nationalism, isolationism, and nativism that's currently wreaking so much damage in countries throughout the world.

But that's not to say that education needs to or should pivot away from the pragmatic goals of a meaningful education. As many mainstream, traditional jobs decline, so too should the traditional learning systems that were focused on training for those jobs. With the development of new work and specialized disciplines, education can shift from its current method of rote learning, where students begin learning from the basics and teachers help them work their way up. Instead, education can become experiential and more focused on students being able to gain applicable, employable skills while in school that can be applied in a fast-evolving work universe.

Education and its components will also have the opportunity to meet these and other challenges by remaining as flexible as possible in content, instruction, and other aspects of the learning process. One overriding reason is that the specifics of the future remain largely unclear. As a Dell Technologies and the Institute for the Future report notes, more than three-quarters of the jobs that will exist in 2030 have yet to be created. That type of uncertainty mandates the capacity to adapt learning materials and methodologies so that the economy of the future isn't spilling over with countless jobs for which relatively few people are qualified.[6]

Greater flexibility also applies to the timeline associated with learning. Rather than devoting the first 20 years or so of a person's life to formal schooling, education will trend toward more informal learning that's adaptable to people of all ages. This ties in closely with shifts in the characteristics of the workforce, as employees who take on more the role of a freelancer or gig worker rather than a lifelong employee locked in the same job will require access to greater lifelong learning opportunities to obtain and sharpen necessary skills as needed.

Fig. 7.2. Photo by Katerina Holmes from Pexels.

These varied opportunities also clearly suggest that teachers will have to change as well. Education at all levels has an opening to recraft education into a more personal, individualized, and self-directed approach. For one thing, a more informed and technologically savvy student population will be able to have more control over what and how they learn. Teachers will increasingly adopt the role of mentors rather than instructors serving up information that students merely memorize, guiding students through more individual and autonomous processes of inquiry and research. One observer has characterized this dynamic as the "flipped classroom"—in effect, students and parents serving as individual leaders of the education process with teachers taking on greater roles as advisors.

Here, artificial intelligence (AI), machine learning, and other forms of technology will prove essential in allowing education to leverage the opportunities inherent in widespread change. On a purely practical level, AI can be used to grade student performance and other administrative responsibilities, thereby freeing up teachers to spend more time on program development and student interaction. AI can also be employed to help tutor students who are struggling with certain basics and fundamentals, leaving human teachers to address more advanced and sophisticated problems.

In these and other areas, education has the opportunity to leverage all the varied technology solutions that were embraced during the COVID-19 pandemic. One leader has phrased it as a "stepping-stone" to even more tech-based solutions, not just a mere temporary adoption. That opportunity will call for genuine commitment formed by thoughtful leadership, along with action geared toward a lasting role for technology rather than the short-term fix mandated by the pandemic. Systemic, long-term planning and execution will be essential.

One obvious tool that will prove critical in leveraging these and other opportunities in education lies in the growing pervasiveness of remote learning. While implemented in response to the pandemic, increased use of technology in education affords the opportunity to "democratize" education—and not just in the capacity to lessen physical boundaries by offering educational resources to more people. The pandemic has highlighted socioeconomic differences in many areas—access to medical care being one such glaring example—but particularly so in education. With the lack of common ground of a brick-and-mortar school—where, for instance, low-income students may have their sole form of access to computers and other tools—education has the opportunity to minimize this disparity by boosting the number of school-provided laptops, increasing bandwidth, and training teachers and staff for greater use of digital education. That, too, will mandate commitment.

DISTANCE LEARNING ORIGINS

My first job in publishing was in the year 2000 at the McGraw-Hill Companies in Los Angeles. I was the designated writer and editor for the reprint cycles of the high school and college accounting textbooks that were distributed throughout the United States. In my first year, management launched a revolutionary (at the time) program dubbed "distance learning." I had to create course outlines and syllabi for teachers to use with students who for one reason or another could not attend classes in person. As this happened more than 20 years ago, Zoom and other platforms we regularly use today were not developed yet. Students and teachers communicated effectively via email or by phone, and those same students reportedly did well in their coursework despite the physical distance between them and their classmates—an early harbinger of how and why distance learning could be so effective.

—Shelley Moench-Kelly

But it's critical to recognize that remote learning isn't a flaw-free panacea. For instance, in higher education, the London-based Economist Intelligence Unit found that 60 percent of college-level faculty reported a drop in engagement in online learning venues as students struggled to stay focused. For their part, 70 percent of faculty expressed concern about their ability to deliver engaging, high-value learning experiences.[7]

But some institutions are responding to these challenges, some very proactively. For instance, Florida State University's "Campus Reimagined" initiative—a program geared to modernizing the overall learning experience—was already in place prior to the onset of the COVID-19 pandemic. One entrepreneurship class led by Professor Bill Lindner, director of the Campus Reimagined program, recorded more than 100 short, on-demand lecture sessions. In class, students used a custom app on their mobile devices to select class content for the day, enabling them to direct their own course of study.[8] Students were encouraged to provide real-time feedback during lectures and received weekly personalized recommendations based on their interests and goals for the course.

Over time, an ongoing cycle of enhanced student engagement and critical feedback on how to improve the class produced high student involvement and satisfaction. Moreover, when the pandemic hit, the class was able to adapt quickly, effectively maintaining a business-as-usual environment. That bodes well for the use of such a model in other settings, whether driven by the necessity of a public health crisis or simply as a matter of routine academic activity.

The varied forms of change and evolution that have and will continue to occur in education raise a central question: Are grades obsolete? Some would argue that they are, particularly given the emphasis on better responding to student desires. After all, who among us enjoyed the prospect of sweating out a grade? Moreover, some would maintain that students in a grade-driven environment are far more focused on the grade itself rather than what's actually being learned—a question more of an ability to memorize and regurgitate than genuinely absorb material.

One possible option with which students can demonstrate proficiency is what's referred to as a "mastery-based approach." Here, rather than writing a research paper or being tested repeatedly, students can be charged with resubmitting work as often as needed until they have shown that they have the material down. The priority is ultimately absorption and comprehension, not fact spitting on demand.

THE JOY OF ONLINE LEARNING

I never finished my undergraduate studies because I have a learning disability and it became too stressful to take the more advanced courses in my junior and senior years to earn my major. In the presence of my fellow students, I felt crushing pressure to perform, and the more I tried, the more I pushed to blend in and learn at the same rate as my peers, the more the system worked against me. I had to drop out. In the last few years, I noticed Ivy League schools were offering remote learning, and that slowly spread to more medium-tier schools. I applied to several universities, some in cities I never could afford to live in, and was accepted at four! Even though I still have nearly two years to go to complete my degree, online learning is so compatible with the way I learn. I feel as if the teachers and I have a one-on-one relationship, and I don't feel pressured by other students. Earning my degree will take the time it takes, and I know I've got the smarts to succeed. Learning today is so different from what I'm used to, which was very militaristic. There was no room for people with learning disabilities or comprehension challenges. Now there is! It's still hard, but psychologically it's more "forgiving" and I am so motivated to succeed.

—N. E., Student, Great Neck, NY

A mastery-focused methodology offers a number of advantages. For one thing, it furthers the focus on experiential learning—rather than sweating out a final or term paper grade, students will come to understand that learning doesn't boil down to a one-shot, sink-or-swim environment. Rather, mastering something often mandates ongoing revision and fine-tuning—an element of real-world life that grade-based education often ignores.

It also underscores a greater focus on and understanding of students' personal well-being. As we all know, grades can be a brutal experience, and not one that necessarily lends itself to better education. If the schools boost their efforts in the future to teach the value of softer skills such as empathy and understanding, why not apply those same parameters to the way students are judged and held accountable?

Interestingly, however, the increased use of certain forms of technology has served to reaffirm the importance of somewhat older tools to maximize the varied opportunities in education. Given many students' struggles to learn via Zoom and other forms of communication, education leaders will be compelled to reexamine the various ways human beings learn and, from there, adjust learning strategies accordingly.

One such "old-school" tool is VARK, an acronym for the four different learning styles discovered by researchers Neil D. Fleming and Coleen E. Mills in 1992. Employing a testing system similar to the well-known Meyers-Briggs personality tests, VARK identifies four principal learning styles—visual, aural (discussion), reading/writing, and kinesthetic (learning by doing, practical exercises, and trial and error).

Throughout the pandemic, teaching at all levels was decidedly challenged by the abrupt shift to remote learning programs, and not just in the technological sense. Given the personal dynamics of in-person instruction, teachers were charged with identifying new and different ways to make school both effective and engaging.

However difficult that forced environment may have been, it's proven beneficial in a number of ways. For one thing, teaching skills and creativity likely improved as a result of the need to connect with students in a remote environment. Additionally, given the varied components available to Zoom instruction, teachers' engagement with all four types of learners likely improved as well. And, lastly, since a project-based, trial-and-error learning environment is growing increasingly popular among students, teachers were able to gain valuable kinesthetic-focused instruction experience that will better equip them to work more effectively with students in more traditional educational settings.

Once again, new and evolving forms of technology can help make education more effective and engaging for students. For instance, the development and growth of virtual reality holds enormous promise for a number of central education objectives. First, given that virtual reality immerses users in a digital environment with which they can interact, students geared to kinesthetic types of learning will likely enjoy and benefit enormously from such hands-on, participatory experiences. For instance, rather than reading or hearing about how a surgeon works, virtual reality affords the opportunity to experience such a profession firsthand. History students can "visit" Ellis Island and other historic portals where their families may have entered the United States.

Other forms of technology are also opening up opportunities for fresh, stimulating education protocols. While often relegated to hobbyists and systems for quick, hands-free delivery of various products, drones are another developing innovation with significant learning potential. Akin to virtual reality, drones offer a highly hands-on, immersive learning experience, such as teaching various laws of physics. Mathematics is another drone-friendly learning topic. For instance, a school in Bangkok is instructing students to learn how to make and read graphs, calculate distances, and understand basic trigonometry principles by tracking and analyzing the paths of different drones—an ideal example of the value and immersion of experiential learning.

Education also has the opportunity to step up and help address growing pervasive problems, many of which have yet to be extensively covered at any educational level. For instance, Stanford University now offers several new majors related to climate change and the environment. One such program is a major known as bioengineering, which trains students at the "interface of life sciences and engineering" and merges expertise and resources in the departments of medicine, biology, and engineering.[9] Additionally, the university has introduced programs and a major in "green chemistry," which combines chemistry, biology, and environmental science to allow students to examine environmental problems such as synthetic fuels, bioplastics, and toxicology, and to train them in pollution reduction methodology.[10]

This is a key area in many ways, but particularly so at the corporate and governmental levels. Although plenty of companies and others are enthusiastic about addressing climate change, many are hindered by the reality that some current employees, having attended school in an earlier era, simply never received sufficient training and education in climate issues. Addressing this shortfall before someone enters the professional world should prove a boon for effective environmental policy-making and subsequent education.

An additional opportunity of enormous significance for education at all levels is strengthening media literacy. Although a basic definition ascribes media literacy to the ability to identify different types of media and understand the accompanying messages, media literacy also includes the skills to access, analyze, evaluate, and create media in a variety of forms.

In one respect, strengthening media literacy is critical to combatting misinformation and other efforts geared to spreading and supporting false or misleading information. Elements such as fact-checking, references, and other strategies and tools can be used effectively to discern genuine news from concocted, ersatz material.

But there are benefits other than boosting the ability to spot fake news. In teaching students systematic means to differentiate between truth and fiction, critical-thinking skills and greater appreciation of perspective are also strengthened. So, too, can media literacy benefit students who will likely create more online content and material than preceding generations. Teaching media literacy adds a component of clear, precise communication, not to mention it is complementary to the importance of approaching technological skills within a moral, ethical framework.

Lastly, media literacy is also consistent with other pervasive changes regarding education in general—in this respect, the notion of ongoing, lifelong learning. Rather than a one-and-done proposition, media literacy is clearly an element of long-term education as technology and content evolve and grow. Moreover, by seeing media literacy as learning that doesn't just take place in the classroom—the so-called partnership involving the classroom and the living room—the idea that education is ongoing and accessible most anywhere is reinforced.

Given the enormous forces driving widespread change, the notion of education as relatively short-term preparation for employment is fast being turned on its head. The same can be said for health care, which stands to turn away from a model more appropriately labeled "sickcare"— the focus of the following chapter.

CHAPTER 7—LEARN AND TRANSFORM

1. Although much of the emphasis regarding ongoing changes in education has to do with technological innovations and advancements, empathy and an accompanying emphasis on the development of so-called soft skills are of equal importance. As students and their families increasingly occupy the role of influential consumers,

education at all levels will need to remain in touch with shifting priorities and interests. An additional component of empathy in education has to do with addressing morality in the use of break-through technology. Students have made it clear that they don't want to know merely how to use sophisticated tech tools but how to do so responsibly and with an awareness for technology's impact on all sorts of people and organizations.

2. The synergy between emerging technology and responsible use underscores the overall shift in education—a change in focus from job training to educating students in a more complete, mean-ingful manner, with content and value that aren't limited to the workplace. In effect, education has the opportunity to mold better citizens, not merely people trained to excel at their jobs.

3. One example of the more "complete" student has to do with media literacy. As fake news, misinformation, and other forms of ersatz material appear in varied forms, it will be critical for students to acquire the analytical skills to better judge legitimacy and rele-vance. The benefits are twofold. On one level, students grow into more informed citizens better equipped to delineate actual news and information from their insidious counterparts. Further, media literacy can contribute to the development of overall communica-tion skills, such as empathy and problem-solving.

4. Technology has certainly opened opportunities inherent in expe-riential forms of learning. Three-dimensional applications, virtual workshops, and other tools have not only boosted the varied alter-natives for experiential learning experiences but likely will boost student engagement as well. "Visiting" a historic site via virtual reality is undoubtedly more compelling than merely reading about it in a dry textbook—a self-evident fact that educators will do well to leverage in every way possible.

5. Online learning can help drive positive change in varied forms but needs to be systemically refined and matured to a more consistently effective and engaging form. In addition to content, class structure, and other elements, online learning should also strive to connect students as much as possible—with the instructors, as well as their fellow students. In one respect, this can be as simple as an instructor asking how their students are doing—nothing to do with school, just how they're feeling and behaving. Systemic development of smaller, more intimate study groups, even though they may take place via Zoom or some other app, can also serve to address the emotional and social needs of students in addition to the purely academic.

CHAPTER 8

THE OPPORTUNITY IN
HEALTH CARE—SHEDDING
A "SICKCARE" SYSTEM

LIKE A COSMETIC SURGERY PATIENT seemingly transformed overnight, health care is going to look radically different in the not-too-distant future. But unlike the recipient of a nose job or tummy tuck, health care's transformation will be anything but superficial.

On one level, exponentially expanding and maturing research and treatment stand to eradicate diseases and conditions that are currently all too commonplace. Cancer, diabetes, and other maladies very likely will join smallpox, polio, and other diseases that have been relegated to the infamous dumpster of medical history. That unto itself is just cause for anticipation and celebration.

But the mechanics, structure, and focus of health care will also undergo dynamic, exponential change. Currently, health care is composed of scattered, disconnected silos, from care providers to pharmaceutical companies to medical equipment manufacturers. While disparate, in one way or another all of these entities are geared primarily to responding to illness and injury—unfortunately, oftentimes in conflict with one another. As one report aptly puts it, the current health-care system is, in fact, essentially a "sickcare" system.[1]

But drivers such as the Fourth Industrial Revolution and the COVID-19 pandemic have positioned health care in its varied permutations to shift that focus to a more unified, proactive, and cost-effective model. And, once again, the consumer is increasingly at the heart of change, particularly with regard to ready access to comprehensive individual health information. Easily shared data, artificial intelligence (AI), and open, secure platforms will continue to merge to create a multilayered and highly specific view of patients' overall well-being and health—one that they can have access to when and how they wish.

That newfound level of individual access and involvement reflects a particularly expansive adoption of technology. Although medicine and health care stand to benefit enormously from technological innovations regarding research and patient treatment, the advantages are not exclusively internal. Rather, as one analysis points out, digital solutions "have the most impact when they extend beyond the walls of an organization and encompass more of its end-to-end value chain"—in other words, making the patient as consumer a cornerstone of a shifting industry.[2]

That changing focus toward the end user can be seen in the increased use of technology to keep patients as informed as possible. Online patient portals—websites that provide ready patient access to medications, test results, upcoming appointments, medical bills, and even price estimates—are now commonplace. Not only are such portals comprehensive in their capacity to let patients review varied aspects of their health care, but they are also greatly shortening the time frame in which patients can receive updates and recent test results. Quickly disappearing are the days when waiting nervously for a phone call or letter was the norm.

BOOSTING RESPONSE TIME

I recently had to undergo tests to rule out a potentially concerning condition. Not only did the results come back with the best news possible, but I also received an email less than two hours after the tests' completion notifying me that the results were available for viewing on the health-care provider's patient portal—sparing me hours and even days of preoccupation. Moreover, I was able to see my test results hours before my family GP reviewed them.

This level of responsiveness has been noticeable in other areas of my relationship with health-care providers. In addition to greater digital access to information regarding my health status, medications, and other aspects, response time from health-care providers has also greatly improved. I no longer hear, "We'll try to get back to you *by the end of the day*." Rather, questions and issues are often addressed within a matter of hours and often exclusively online. I doubt my evident experience of being treated as much like a consumer as a patient is an outlier.

—Jeff Wuorio

But exponential growth of technology in health care isn't limited to the sharing of information and data. Consistent with trends toward a greater emphasis on proactivity and prevention, portability in a variety of forms, such as health trackers and wearables, is another significant feature of exponential change. Mobile technology's advantages include helping with chronic disease management, providing safety and security for elderly patients, and extending service to chronically underserved areas. Perhaps most valuable of all is the expected cost savings. A Brookings Institution analysis found that remote monitoring technologies could save as much as $197 billion over the next 25 years by identifying illness early, enabling proactive intervention and furthering research into greater understanding of disease progression.[3]

DIGITIZING HEALTH CARE

When it comes to innovating business models for health-care delivery, it appears we have failed to keep pace with clinical advances, and surprisingly with most other industries.

Here I want to share with you, in part, what I wrote in one of my books, *Sustained Innovation* (2007) about this very topic.[4] Although some of the data I am sharing here may have changed slightly since the book was first published, the fundamentals remain the same.

Let's analyze the health-care delivery system from the perspective of information flows. We have a wide variety of players: doctors, hospitals, insurance companies, employers, government, and researchers, all operating in an environment that makes up a complex supply chain. And for this complex supply chain, transparent business models and processes need to be established to enable collaboration.

Health-care services have spent less than one-tenth what banks and other industries have spent on technology investments to create better information flow and cross-boundary collaboration. Various studies have yielded this alarming picture:

- Every year, medical errors cause 98,000 deaths (some studies suggest the number is twice that) and one million injuries.
- Medical errors kill more people each year than breast cancer, AIDS, or motor vehicle accidents.
- Thirty to forty percent of the money we spend on health care—more than half a trillion dollars a year—is spent on costs associated with "overuse, underuse, misuse, duplication, system failures, unnecessary repetition, poor communication and inefficiency."
- One-fifth of medical errors are due to the lack of immediate access to patient information.
- Some 80 percent of medical errors were initiated by miscommunication, including missed communication between physicians, misinformation in medical records, mishandling of patient requests and messages, inaccessible records, mislabeled specimens, misfiled or missing charts, and inadequate reminder systems.

- Three out of every 10 tests are reordered because results cannot be found. Patient charts cannot be found on 30 percent of visits.

- The problem is that vital information is missing throughout the entire supply chain. What information is available must be transferred laboriously by paper; databases in hospitals and doctors' offices are often unable to talk to each other, because there are no data standards.

In some settings, doctors and nurses spend as much time on paperwork as they do treating patients. Did you know that the 130,000 pages of Medicaid and Medicare rules and regulations are three times the size of the Internal Revenue Code? Did you know that a Medicare patient arriving at the emergency room must sign eight different forms?

When all of this is resolved, and we think it will be eventually, the real innovation will not be about new health-care technology or policy. It will be how the medical community rewires the way it works and collaborates by innovating business models with streamlined organization, processes, and automation.

We have to start believing that patients should have access to their medical records and be full participants in the health-care process. This means that health-care services must maintain systems that provide full accessibility to physicians, clinicians, and patients respectively.

Legacy health records and medical delivery systems were never designed for transparency and portability. Actually, they were designed precisely with the opposite intent. The result has been a collective system that isolates information from the people who need it to make faster, better decisions.

This chaos literally costs billions of dollars annually in bloated health-care expenses.

For example, today a hospital can easily develop better patient information management that gives better control over the dissemination of patient data and expedites decision-making, resulting in the following:

continued

- Reduced patient errors through electronic physician order entry
- Elimination of transcription errors
- Reduced pharmacy errors because all prescriptions are sent electronically
- Reduced dosing errors in pediatrics, where dosing is calculated by weight and age
- Lower costs and better outcomes

We are accustomed today to seeing twice as many office staff as medical personnel in a doctor's office. That will change. There will be fewer visits to the doctor; information will be exchanged electronically. There will be fewer repeat tests. Doctors on rounds in a hospital will have everything they need to know in a small device hanging on their belts. Patients will have access to their medical records online, and so will the emergency room. But all this will require change, and change is not easy.

Actually, we already have the technology we need. For example, we already have electronic health records, which capture every piece of information about a patient and are accessible to qualified medical personnel online. In an emergency, the patient doesn't have to remember drugs they're taking, and nobody has to track down a manila folder.

Nevertheless, when studies indicate that only about half of all patients get widely accepted and uncontroversial advice from their doctors—such as taking aspirin for heart conditions—it's time we consider something new. Moreover, if we had a national, intraoperative, medical information network, we would be able to see patterns in the aggregate data. We could learn, for example, whether a certain test is actually worthwhile in a certain situation. The quality of health care would go up and the cost would go down.

Although some progressive health-care providers have begun to transition to digitization, enabling faster and more complete access to patient data, we still have a long way to go toward achieving seamless process and business innovation in health care.

—Faisal Hoque

The ever-increasing range of remote and mobile monitoring devices is striking. Although such devices might often be most readily associated with tracking overall health measurements and monitoring conditions, other applications are far more specific. For instance, researchers at the University of Massachusetts Medical School have developed remote monitoring devices called iHeal for substance abusers. Patients wear sensors that monitor skin temperature and nervous system activities associated with drug cravings. From there, the devices transmit data to health providers, which can offer varied forms of interventions focused on discouraging drug use.[5]

The number of health-care apps that effectively transform cell phones into central elements of individual health care is just as striking in its exponential growth. As of the first quarter of 2021, one estimate held that there was a total of 53,979 health-care apps available in the Apple App Store, almost double the number from the same time frame in 2015.[6]

Although physicians were formerly reluctant to adopt technology such as electronic health records, their enthusiasm for and support of portable health-care devices is evident. More than four out of five doctors are in full support of patients tracking their health at home, using different kinds of health apps, particularly for weight management, blood sugar levels, and monitoring vital signs.[7] This also strengthens a commitment to more proactive, anticipatory health care rather than a system geared almost exclusively to treatment and maintenance after the fact.

With a technological "foothold" in consumers' ready adoption of wearable health-tracking devices, industry observers suggest the next generation will also incorporate discreet health sensors in devices located throughout homes and other areas. One example might be a bathroom mirror equipped with sensors to identify changes in moles on a person's skin. Additionally, such at-home health-tracking setups could monitor certain aspects of a patient's physical appearance and track shifts in appearance that relate to cardiovascular health problems—skin color changes that can reflect certain blood flow dynamics that are indicative of cardiovascular health.

Varied technological advances and innovation also afford an opportunity to boost the speed at which patients receive treatment should that prove necessary. Rather than a patient falling ill, making an appointment, and receiving tests, diagnosis, and then treatment, ongoing monitoring of a patient's health can identify issues sooner, as well as expedite whatever care they may need. The growing use of telehealth services further boosts health care's rapidly growing capacity to accelerate response and treatment.

One obvious challenge to this level of proactivity is the issue of privacy—the fear that, having taken your job, robots and machines now "want to see what you do when you're in the bathroom." Consistent with other forms of technological evolution, this will challenge health-care providers to not only demonstrate the efficacy of such technology but also reassure patients that the information will be managed securely, as well as ethically—still another call to action regarding the crossover between technology and moral, responsible use.

THE PROACTIVE PATIENT

I've had adult-onset type 2 diabetes for 19 years, controlling it with oral medication. When that medication's efficacy began to drop, my primary care physician put me on insulin. I gained 30 pounds in two months' time and my numbers only dropped by 5 percent. A dear friend who's a holistic/naturopathic practitioner suggested I "eat clean" and stop the insulin immediately. By eating clean, she meant no rice, pasta, bread, or anything that turned to sugar. No processed foods. "Shop the perimeter," she insisted, meaning that I should keep to fresh produce and proteins. Within one week, my blood sugars were normal and I was off all medication. Within seven weeks, I lost 30 pounds and my blood sugar readings dropped to a normal range, where they remain to this day (six years later). It just goes to show that taking the step to be a proactive patient was definitely a positive one. Now, I keep in touch with my doctor between visits via patient portals, and it's as if she's my friend and mentor. Gone are the days of waiting a year between physicals or weeks for an appointment to check something out.

—Shelley Moench-Kelly

Shelley's story also reinforces another opportunity for health care in an era of change—a more informed and educated patient. While 20 years ago, an informed patient might be described as one who read an article—quite likely outdated—about joint pain in a doctor's waiting room, internet access now affords patients of all ages and differing levels of health the opportunity to learn from such unquestioned authorities as the Minnesota-based Mayo Clinic and Johns Hopkins University in Baltimore, Maryland. Although jokes about diagnosing oneself via Google may abound, greater digital access can better prepare patients to understand what their doctors tell them and to ask more valuable, pertinent questions. It's hard to imagine any health-care worker who wouldn't embrace an intelligent, reasoned patient base.

Social media is also playing its part in boosting access to a proliferation of useful data and information. Doctors once only known in their hometowns have become media darlings with streams of instructional YouTube videos. For example, "Dr. Mike," Mike Varshavski, is a family medicine specialist in Manhattan with more than six million YouTube followers. Dr. Ed Hope's channel, "Dr. Hope's Sick Notes"—where the former advertising executive turned emergency medical doctor entertains and enlightens viewers with useful, relatable information—has nearly 500,000 followers.

Technology and AI are also transforming how hospitals and other health-care facilities function internally. Major hospitals are already

THE ROBOT WILL SEE YOU NOW

I'm in my 40s and last year started having gastric discomfort. I'm otherwise in very good health. My doctor diagnosed me with gallstones and ordered gallbladder removal. I always remembered the image of former president Lyndon B. Johnson showing off his horrendous 10-inch scar across his belly and the horror stories from my uncle about his eight-week recovery from gallbladder surgery. The thoughts of either weren't welcome, but I knew I had to do something or risk further damage. I shared my concerns with my doctor, who smiled patiently at me and patted me on the arm. He said, "It's all done by me and a robot. You'll have four small incisions, and you can go home the next day." He was right. I was shocked, but happily so!

—G. M., Accountant, Berkeley, CA

employing AI-enabled systems to augment medical staff in patient diagnosis and treatment activities for a wide range of diseases. AI systems are also making an impact on improving the efficiency of nursing and managerial activities of hospitals—not dissimilar to AI's use in education to help teachers grade papers and perform other forms of housekeeping.

Not surprisingly, technology is also transforming how procedures such as surgery are carried out. Use of robotics in a variety of surgeries is expanding rapidly. Robot-assisted procedures accounted for 15.1 percent of all general surgeries in 2018, up from less than 2 percent in 2012, according to a 2020 study.[8] In particular, the use of robotics tools is becoming more prevalent in hernia operations, reflux surgery, cardiac surgery, and other procedures.

Proponents of robotic surgery point to a number of advantages, including minimal invasiveness, greater surgical accuracy, lowered chances of infection and other complications, and reduced hospital stays. However, not only do others question the purported benefits of robotic surgery, but also the cost of such technology is consistently more expensive than more traditional procedures (certain attachments that go on the end of robotic arms are disposable, which can boost the cost of robotic procedures by thousands of dollars). To fully realize the opportunity and potential of robotic procedures, associated costs will have to be reduced to make the technology more financially viable. That may occur when robotic surgeries and procedures become more commonplace, removing a degree of exclusivity from their use and trimming consumer cost.

Another area ripe with opportunity is the discipline known as nanoscience, the study of exceedingly small materials (a page from a newspaper is roughly 100,000 nanometers thick). Researchers have found that individual nano materials have properties that are very different from what they display when joined together. As a result, research is ongoing to explore the use of nano materials that can be used to detect very small particles or bacteria. If effective, the technology will strengthen early diagnostic efforts and more proactive, less invasive treatment.

Fig. 8.1. Photo by ThisIsEngineering from Pexels.

Further, certain technological advances will go beyond transforming disease treatment and prevention, effectively identifying cures for certain diseases. For example, gene-editing technologies have the potential to cure genetic diseases, such as sickle cell disease and cystic fibrosis. Germline editing—the process by which the genome of a patient is edited in sperm cells or female eggs—can possibly cure diseases with permanent intergenerational changes. Additionally, somatic genome editing—those cells that affect a person's body alone—can treat, control, and possibly cure acquired diseases.

This segues into several other types of opportunity that, in their own way, are more global than some other medical innovations and advancement. For one thing, the overall shift toward the individual as consumer, proactivity, and other similar trends underscore a growing focus on complete well-being, not merely cures. The future of health care will emphasize the totality of the consumer's health, rather than merely identifying and treating illness, including physical health, as well as mental, social, emotional, and spiritual health. Health care's continued movement toward illness prevention and health maintenance, rather than merely responding to sickness, will further patients' mental and emotional well-being by reducing anxiety, uncertainty, and time spent waiting for test results and other data of concern.

Just as valuable, health-care data captured in real time can generate new knowledge and evidence to better understand patterns of health and disease. Access to real-world evidence will play a critical role in the development of what is referred to as a "living health system." Here, data from ongoing health-care activities are continuously aggregated and analyzed. Subsequent research and analysis are incorporated into improving future care, creating a system in which "science, informatics, incentives and culture are aligned for continuous improvement and innovation, with best practices seamlessly embedded in the delivery process and new knowledge captured as an integral by-product of the delivery experience."[9]

This more closely coordinated and comprehensive gathering of medical information and research will prove particularly critical with regard to the outbreak of future pandemics and other widespread public health issues. COVID has shown in the starkest terms possible not merely the consequences of lack of proactive preparedness with regard to response and treatment but also the dangers of disconnected entities attempting to coordinate their efforts. Add to that the medical community's responsibility to aid in the effort to counteract misinformation, a practice that, again—we have seen all too graphically—can measure its so-called success with a body count. The presence of such iconic, trusted names, such as the Mayo Clinic and a number of well-known universities, may offer health care a slight advantage over other areas when it comes to combatting false medical information and advice. Hopefully, brand names still carry clout and credibility.

Obviously, the elephant in the room with regard to any discussion of the future of health care is consumer costs. With some 6 out of 10 Americans dealing with some form of chronic disease (and 4 out of 10 coping with two or more), hospital care now makes up about one-third of all health-care spending in the United States. Chronic illnesses are tied to more than 80 percent of hospital admissions.[10]

A greater focus on proactive and preventive health care can help reverse that. Tracking various elements of health 24/7 and identifying health risks earlier will result in fewer and less severe diseases. That can significantly trim health-care spending. Further savings can be achieved through technology. With such tools as telehealth, consumers will have the cost-effective alternative of dealing with many routine health matters at home—leaving expensive specialists free to treat more complicated, involved health issues.

Drugs and medications are another area where opportunity exists to trim costs significantly. Drug companies are now employing AI to identify the most effective form of drugs for particular diseases. For example,

Atomwise, a company that develops AI systems, partnered with the University of Toronto and IBM by supplying an algorithm to research treatments for the Ebola virus. Not only did the algorithm identify two effective drugs, but the analysis also took less than a day as opposed to months or even years with more typical research methods.[11]

It's a gross understatement to say that health care and medicine have their work cut out for them in trying to wrestle consumer costs into even a semblance of control. For example, the cost of genome sequencing has fallen below $1,000. On the other hand, while there are tens of thousands of new drugs in the pipeline, some of which have already had a profound impact in developing cures, particularly in cancer, many carry staggering costs. For example, recently developed forms of cell therapy can cost more than $1 million for one treatment for a single patient.[12]

Fortunately, the integration of various tools and approaches—including wearables, sensors, big data, AI, augmented reality, nanotechnology, and robotics, among others—can serve as a foundation for value-based care approaches and payment models, focusing on improving individual outcomes while trimming the cost of care for individual patients. By improving both end results and efficiency, the health-care system can reduce redundancies and waste, which by some estimates account for up to one-third of the current total spent for health care.

But these and the other varied opportunities in medicine and health care will mandate dramatically different mindsets and approaches to fully leverage this exponential level of change. For one thing, health care at all levels should ready itself for ongoing, constant disruption. For instance, health-care providers will be compelled to embrace virtual care as much as possible—again, largely in response to growing consumer acceptance and use.

In a 2019 Gallup survey, only 14 percent of Americans said they had used telemedicine in the past year, with only 17 percent expecting to use it in 2020. But by March 2020, 34 percent of Americans reported having used telemedicine, with nearly half saying they are likely to use it in the future—almost three times greater than approximately six months prior.[13]

Greater use of telemedicine also underscores the move toward totality and coordination of care. Hospitals and other health-care providers will need to constantly monitor patient information across a spectrum of care and venues, including digital. Effective integration and management of this data will mandate flexible proactive leadership, as well as significant investment in infrastructure and capacity.

That will also require far greater cooperation and partnerships than have characterized health care in the past. Rather than the largely autonomous "silos" that composed health care, proactive collaboration among players in an evolving new ecosystem will be critical in transforming health care and improving accessibility.

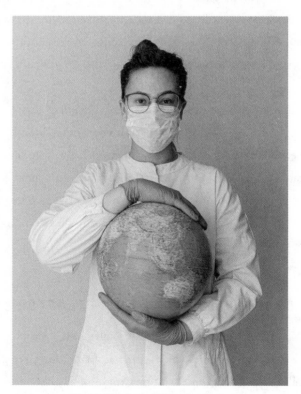

Fig. 8.2. Photo by Anna Shvets from Pexels.

That cooperation and interaction should extend beyond traditional providers and other players. Technology giants, start-ups, and other disruptors that are new to the health-care universe are generally motivated and positioned to drive meaningful change. What they don't have is health-care expertise, regulatory experience, and existing partnerships with other incumbents. As a result, disruptors will likely be eager to partner with existing entities whom they view as equally focused on driving innovation.

Overall, the health-care opportunities of tomorrow will hinge on developing and leveraging what can be referred to as the overall health-care "ecosystem." As the industry as a whole moves toward greater collaboration and partnerships, individual stakeholders will capture opportunity by close coordination with new technologies, providers, and other players, both those who are established and the Johnny-come-latelies. Leaders in this ecosystem—including government, private enterprise, and other entities—should be committed to the common goal of transforming health care and improving accessibility while also offering unique and singular contributions to that effort.

These and other efforts and developments should ultimately be geared to appealing to the newly empowered health consumer. Stakeholders need to engage effectively with consumers while working to earn their trust and demonstrate value. Genuinely understanding that the dynamics of health care have shifted toward the individual marks the first step in strengthening consumers' faith and confidence that the care they're receiving is not only effective but also as cost conscious as possible.

CHAPTER 8—LEARN AND TRANSFORM

1. Health care needs to systemically evolve into a more closely coordinated industry in which partners of all sorts cooperate and collaborate much more than they traditionally have done. This can

include everyone from the health-care industry itself to pharmaceutical manufacturers to insurance companies. Technology such as AI and other like developments will make such a confluence that much more viable to assemble, not to mention better positioned to analyze and subsequently apply conclusions and breakthroughs. Further, technology such as patient portals and other tools can make more complete and detailed information that much more readily available to patients.

2. Health care also needs to be empathetic to the needs and priorities of greatly empowered consumers. This dovetails with a growing emphasis on complete well-being, not necessarily just the physical. Similar to the synergy and cooperation outlined in the prior point, this will mandate closer cooperation between all sorts of health-care providers, including physicians, therapists (both physical and otherwise), and others. Technology can also help to boost the efficiency and efficacy of such cooperation, not to mention involve patients in a more ongoing, comprehensive manner.

3. Proactivity, not merely response to illness or injury, is an enormous opportunity in health care, given the fast-expanding proliferation of research, wearables, and other means of pinpointing health issues at an earlier and more affordable stage. By leveraging technology and other applications geared to ongoing monitoring and early identification, greater levels of proactive health care will likely not only produce better patient outcomes but also reduce consumer costs as expensive and prolonged treatment for more advanced conditions become less common.

4. One central challenge to incorporating technology to increase proactive health care is privacy. Put simply, patients will need to feel comfortable with a certain degree of ongoing observation, as well as confident in the security of their proprietary information.

Here, simple experiential learning should be applied. The medical community undoubtedly is aware that many patients are gun-shy when it comes to widespread technology—and why. Both those realities should be systematically applied to solutions geared to lessening patient anxiety and, as a result, boosting participation to make the most of the opportunity to know more and respond more quickly.

CHAPTER 9

THE OPPORTUNITY IN THE
PUBLIC SECTOR—THE RISE OF
THE "DIGITAL CITIZEN"

THE OPPORTUNITY AFFORDED by change in the public sector is enormous. It's also a bit ironic.

On the one hand, like business and so many other institutions, government by its very nature resists change. In many ways, the processes by which government operates haven't changed very much in decades and even longer. On the other, technological innovation, coupled with the immediacy of the COVID-19 pandemic, has amply demonstrated the need for government at all levels to adapt and change both quickly and substantially.

And therein lies the opportunity.

As is the case with most every other aspect of life, government now serves a citizen population that is far more informed and—ideally, at least—involved in the areas of governance and public services in a positive and productive manner (hence the inclusion of "ideally"). And, like everything from health care to education, these empowered citizens can best be seen as consumers—end users who have every right to expect a high return from what they invest in taxes and other forms of financial support for government.

That's a healthy form of synergy in many ways. On the one hand, increasing pressure from the citizenry on government to perform better, faster, and more efficiently will likely prove a powerful catalyst for productive change. And, like a customer at a particular store who returns to shop again and again following a positive experience, a government that offers top-tier, responsive service can satisfy citizens that their money is being well spent, as well as induce them to greater levels of involvement and support—particularly financially, if or when that becomes necessary.

That could prove a timely, advantageous development. Not surprisingly, citizens are less than thrilled with the current performance of government. According to a recent Gallup poll, roughly a mere one-quarter of Americans are satisfied with the nation's system of government and the quality of its operations and services. More specifically, the poll conducted in January 2021 found only 27 percent of people polled expressed satisfaction, down from 43 percent from the prior year. That high level of disapproval is higher than in any prior year in the past two decades of Gallup polls.[1]

Admittedly, the timing of that particular poll was bound to produce those sorts of discouraging results, coming as it did amid the January 6, 2021, attempted insurrection at the US Capitol, the then-president Trump's administration's ongoing and aggressive fallacies about the election results, and continuing frustration regarding response to the COVID-19 pandemic. Nonetheless, despite those factors, it's evident that government has a great deal to do to boost its standing with citizens.

Moreover, just "good enough" will no longer be sufficient to improve citizen approval of government to a meaningful degree. Like other areas impacted by change, the bar has been set exceedingly high, if for no other reason than those citizens who wish to be as fully informed as possible now have technology at their disposal to make that easier and more comprehensive than ever before. Government is anything but the exception. Further, as was pointed out earlier, governmental institutions are by their very nature somewhat gun-shy about implementing change, let alone change that is fast moving and expanding exponentially.

That's one highly discouraging characteristic of the Fourth Industrial Revolution as it relates to necessary change in government. As former US secretary of state Madeleine Albright has observed, government is tasked with understanding and responding to a range of 21st-century challenges equipped with 20th-century mindsets and 19th-century institutions.[2] Government must acknowledge that change and disruption are occurring much faster and in more complex forms than ever before.

FASTER BENEFITS

I first filed for unemployment in 1990 when my company laid off employees to prepare for a corporate sale. Back then, filers had to physically go to the unemployment office and wait in lines just as you do at the DMV. Filers were interviewed by staff and designated as eligible or not eligible to receive claim benefits. The problem was, nobody told filers that at the time. We had to wait for a few weeks to receive the benefit notifications in snail mail. Every two weeks, we had to fill out paper forms and mail them back to the processing centers and wait another week or so to receive a paper check. Nowadays, everything (including appeals) is done online, and you can access the system at any time to catch up on your claim status, contact your local unemployment department, file initial claims, or cancel a claim. I'm sure most in the younger generations wouldn't believe such an antiquated system that so many of us had to deal with way back when even existed in their lifetimes.

—Shelley Moench-Kelly

The challenges and opportunity that government confronts, as the World Economic Forum has phrased it, can be boiled down to how well it can evolve into an entity characterized as adaptive, human-centered, inclusive, and capable of producing sustainable policies and practices—in so many words, both empathetic and responsive. And, as will be discussed later in this chapter, that challenge will likely not be met if government attempts to achieve all it can without the assistance and involvement of others.

Fig. 9.1. Photo by Canva Studio from Pexels.

One of the first challenges faced by government at all levels is suitable training and preparation to introduce and manage all sorts of innovative, technology-focused means of governance. Not surprisingly, the increased prevalence of new tools and systems in government has caused a fair amount of anxiety among those charged with using them. Currently, there is a glaring lack of such necessary training, a situation made all the more unnerving by the ongoing and exponentially growing transformation of government.

To fully realize the opportunities inherent in this change, governments will need to create comprehensive training and development programs, particularly technological knowledge that will allow managers to handle high volumes of digital information. As citizens' understanding and use of technology grows as well, governments will need to maintain ongoing training for public servants, not only to keep them up to speed with new innovations from a technical standpoint but also to help them better respond to citizens' shifting needs and priorities.

TECHNOLOGY—A GOVERNMENTAL MUST

The US government is the world's largest consumer of technology, spending some $80 billion-plus each year, with much of it wasted on idle servers, systems, and websites dedicated to various departments and offices.[3] Since the dot-com era of the early aughts, the Clinton, Bush, and Obama administrations have made technology-driven innovation a priority in domestic agendas. Politicians and bureaucrats see technology as a giant panacea for inefficient government functions ranging from health care and social services to homeland security and national defense.

Innovation and technology drives everything from education to economic growth. It costs more money to run an inefficient agency, and the system not only fails the people it's meant to serve but eventually hurts them as well. The United States must modernize and innovate rapidly and continually to stay ahead of the developing world, where progress comes quickly. We don't have to look further back than the 2012 presidential election and the devastation caused

continued

by Hurricane Sandy to find opportunities for improvement and change. Consider the following examples:

Big Data and the Big Win: After a database-driven 2008 campaign, Obama's 2012 reelection campaign manager Jim Messina proposed a new metric-driven effort, saying, "We are going to measure every single thing in this campaign." Messina brought in an analytics department five times bigger than the 2008 team, replete with a chief scientist for the Chicago headquarters named Rayid Ghani, whose number-crunching experience includes maximizing the efficiency of supermarket sales promotions. Campaign spokesman Ben LaBolt kept mum on the specifics, claiming, "They are our nuclear codes." On November 4, senior campaign advisors shared their high-tech efforts with *Time* on the condition that they remain anonymous and that the information not be published until after the decision was final. Those included an overhaul of targeting TV ads and complex models of swing-state voters to improve the efficiency of everything from phone calls and front-door visits to direct mailings and social media. Call lists were compiled based on age, sex, race, neighborhood, and voting record, as well as consumer data. "In the end, modeling became something way bigger for us in '12 than in '08 because it made our time more efficient," one senior advisor told *Time* about the predictive profiles based on the data.[4]

Deadly Damages: Superstorm Sandy demonstrated major deficiencies in both the private- and public-sector enterprises that provide basic services and protections to the people. Sandy left about 8.5 million electric customers without service in 21 states after slamming the New Jersey coast on October 29, and none were harder hit than customers served by New York State–owned Long Island Power Authority (LIPA). More than 1 million of LIPA's 1.1 million customers lost power due to deadly Sandy, while 123,000 more, including thousands of whom had had their power restored after Sandy, were knocked out by a subsequent nor'easter. New York governor Andrew Cuomo said November 8 that LIPA's management had failed, and he "will make every change necessary to ensure it lives up to its public responsibility," including removing management. LIPA chief operating officer and acting CEO Michael Hervey resigned on

November 13, the same day Cuomo said he would form a special state commission to probe response by the utility.

Tech Troubles Deter Democracy: Another election, another litany of electronic voting machine misfires and malfunctions across the country, along with a slew of complaints over voter ID laws. Something as vital as a presidential election shouldn't be left to antiquated systems that fail time and again. Without a major technological overhaul and upgrade, many of these legacy systems will continue to cause embarrassing and easily avoidable problems. Some 5,000 lawyers and 3,000 grassroots poll watchers from the nonprofit machine watchdog group Verified Voting documented e-voting machine mess-ups in many states in 2012, including Virginia, Florida, Pennsylvania, and Colorado, which still used direct-recording electronic machines without paper backup for recounts. Barbara Arnwine, executive director of the Lawyers' Committee for Civil Rights Under Law, said voter ID laws were the source of the lawsuits filed over the election, and a hotline set up by advocacy groups had more than 71,000 calls, mostly from states with "trend lines" showing major confusion over voter ID rules. Nine states had laws requiring voters show a state-issued ID, and 17 states required voters to present some kind of photo ID. The United States should take a lesson from India, the first country to build a high-tech database of personal biometric identities for nearly a billion people. India's poor who lack paper proof of their existence were the first in the world able to validate their identities anytime, anywhere in a few seconds. The groundbreaking Indian system surpassed those operated by the FBI and the US visa program.

FOUR PRINCIPLES OF "GOVERNING" INNOVATION

No government official or business leader can assume technology will cure their organization's woes. All forms of innovation and technology require intent and direction to produce a proper, valuable outcome.

continued

A coherent and disciplined management approach is important for several reasons:

Technology Fuels Force and Efficiency: In the private sector, it's a means for gaining a competitive advantage in the marketplace and creating wealth. In the public sector, it's a tool for creating efficiencies in government organizations, which lead to better services for citizens. In all cases, management must implement initiatives to exploit strategic opportunities in which technology can enable innovation and ensure programs are executed with the highest outcome at the lowest cost.

Management of Technology Is More Important Than Technology Itself: The value in productivity improvements must converge investments in technology with innovations in business practices. In government, a program of continuing synergistic improvement initiatives will outpace any single investment in technology, or any innovation in process or practice. An agency-wide perspective is required to ensure that specific technology and change initiatives are being managed as part of an overall program of productivity enhancement.

Real ROI: Maximizing return on capital requires oversight of how well assets are deployed to generate stakeholder value. In government, this refers to the design and execution of technology implementations that produce a cost savings or improved service delivery. The Internal Revenue Service implementing computer services that enable the electronic filing of personal tax returns both increased service delivery and reduced operational expenses. Governance prevents precious and limited budget resources from being expended on programs that lead nowhere.

Managing Risk with Governance: The strategic importance of information and the nature of current technologies have raised the stakes regarding privacy, security, and confidentiality. It's vital that organizational leadership appreciate the material risks inherent in the creation and use of technology. Governance through management policies and procedures ensures that risk is accepted, assigned, or deferred.

A COLLABORATIVE ROAD MAP FOR SUCCESS

The public sector is as tied to the needs of the private market as it is to its constituency. Every major organization in today's complex and constantly changing marketplace requires collaborative execution. As with the private sector, all government agencies are functioning within a global marketplace.

Clearly defining the mission and vision of a public-sector department or agency, effectively creating and communicating a road map to achieve the desired outcomes and then validating the actual results, sounds simple. Yet many government agencies display only limited success in creating an environment that reinforces the development of strategic goals through processes that organize and align their activities in support of achieving goals.

Senior agency executives must understand how technology can lead to improvements in operations and enhanced decision-making. They need practical ways to decide when to invest, how to channel investments, and how to ensure that investments lead to value.

Just as a company bears responsibility in answering to the company shareholders, a government agency must be accountable to its stakeholders—the citizens that depend on critical services. At the end of the day, how a country is managed is by far the most important operation of all.

—Faisal Hoque

Artificial intelligence (AI) is one cornerstone of this evolving digital government. AI affords the opportunity to transform planning, problem-solving, and public services. For instance, the city of Pittsburgh has adopted AI-enabled traffic lighting, which has cut travel times by 25 percent and idling times by 40 percent.[5] Other areas where AI can prove advantageous include optimization of public transportation; air and pollution monitoring; oversight of public garbage and recycling programs; and general public safety, such as nighttime pedestrian traffic.

As has been evident throughout the COVID-19 pandemic, as well as other widespread public events and issues, government can be as vulnerable to misinformation and potentially dangerous false news as any other entity. Witness the pervasive and relentless attacks against public mandates for masks, vaccinations, lockdowns, and other steps that should be viewed as medical imperatives rather than harbingers of supposed conspiracies.

AI can be exceedingly effective when employed to counteract this and other forms of online misinformation. Employing such investigative parameters as repeated use of sensational words and analyzing a website's reputation, AI can quickly pinpoint suspicious activity and respond. For instance, from March through the November 2020 presidential election, Facebook posted warnings for more than 180 million pieces of content on the platform that had been discredited by third-party fact-checkers. Governments of all sorts can employ similar technology. If nothing else, a systematic, coordinated effort to dilute the impact of misinformation could go a long way toward helping to reestablish public trust in government.[6]

Similar to trends in health care, government has the chance to boost systems that provide more anticipatory governance. Tools using data analytics, scenarios, and simulations are allowing governments to identify problems long before they become significant crises. For example, Durham, North Carolina, has employed predictive policing for a number of years, reducing violent crime at a far higher rate than many other comparably sized cities.[7] The accumulation of extensive data can allow AI systems to predict and urge proactive steps in other areas, including interventions for people most likely to be impacted by the opioid crisis or veterans most likely to face housing insecurity before they are actually living on the streets.

AI also holds great promise for government activities on a national level. Of particular value are techniques such as machine learning, computer vision, speech recognition, and robotics. For example, with regard to issues such as national security, natural language processing automatically pinpoints relevant information from intelligence sources and establishes connections. As a result, analysts are that much better positioned to identify accurate and useful material. Additionally, cyber anomaly detection can revolutionize cybersecurity strategies in government systems.

Fig. 9.2. Photo by Negative Space from Pexels.

Another boon of AI is its use to free up government employees— theoretically at least, even at the most local level—from rudimentary and often mundane responsibilities. For instance, human employees inevitably take a great deal of time to manually process large amounts of data, particularly the massive sets collected by the military, aerospace, and other government sectors. But AI completes time-consuming—and tedious— tasks quickly and accurately.

As a result, government workers are freed up to devote their time and energy to other responsibilities. For example, the United States

Citizenship and Immigration Services uses a computer-generated virtual assistant named Emma to answer questions and direct individuals to the right area of the bureau's website. Should further information and clarification prove necessary, a government employee can step in.

AI can also play a significant role in military matters. These include improving situational awareness and decision-making; increasing the safety of equipment such as aircraft, ships, and vehicles in dangerous situations; and predicting when critical parts will fail, automating diagnosis, and scheduling routine maintenance. AI also helps improve the nautical, terrain, and aeronautical charting vital to Department of Defense missions, helping enable safe and precise navigation and more comprehensive surveillance.

One fairly recent example of the application of AI in the military was a comprehensive experiment in 2021 known as the Global Information Dominance Experiments. The exercise combined AI, cloud computing sensors, and other technology that, say military officials, holds the promise of building the capacity to predict significant military activities days in advance—and in a fraction of the time required by human analysts to study and break down the same amount of data.

Government also has the opportunity to utterly transform how its varied services are delivered to citizens. One example of this is what's labeled "no touch government"—where services are automatically provided without the need of a citizen's request. For instance, parents of newborns in Austria don't need to do anything to begin receiving a state-provided financial allowance. Instead, the birth triggers varied transfers of data that eventually end up in local tax offices where funds are disbursed.[8]

Policy-making is still another area ripe with promise. As is the case with so much to do with government, policy makers are often overwhelmed by information that needs to be verified and placed into context before the development of actual policy can even begin. Further complicating this challenge is the presence of lobbyists—highly funded individuals and groups with specific priorities far too often out of line with the public's best interests.

Not only will AI and related technology allow policy makers to better manage and analyze growing amounts of valuable data, but technology also affords new venues in which proposed policies and other governmental actions can be simulated and carried out—so-called regulatory sandboxes. Not only does that permit detailed study of the impact and ramifications of such potential decisions, but also the fact that such analysis can be carried out as a harmless dry run lets government fully dissect policy, legislation, and other steps before they actually go into effect.

These activities have already been implemented, even on a national level. For example, Sweden was able to create a regulatory sandbox to test autonomous vehicles in Gothenburg without the necessity of adjusting either national laws or those of the European Union to accommodate such testing.[9]

Those emerging tools will also prove valuable in heading off what's often referred to as "policy decay"—a term that can take in anything from a law's growing lack of relevance to current conditions to the gradual breakdown of policy goal consensus, among other issues. Again, by being able to test new laws and adjustments before they're actually put into place, governments will be that much more ready to respond systemically to changing needs and priorities—and to respond that much faster should laws and regulations become outdated over time.

A willingness to embrace and implement technology also affords government at all levels the opportunity to be that much more competitive with regard to fostering economic growth and development. For example, in Estonia, the "e-Estonia" initiative serves as a government-operated incubator for breakthrough ideas concerning digital citizenship, security, virtual business, and education. On a more local level, the city of Boston has partnered with the World Economic Forum to investigate the use of autonomous vehicles to reduce vehicular accidents throughout the city.

While eminently pragmatic, the program also serves to showcase Boston as a forward-thinking metropolitan area interested in and receptive to all sorts of technological possibilities.

That can prove a model for other communities. Leveraging AI and other tools, government can help attract investment and other financial activities by positioning itself as business friendly, ranging from top-tier technological infrastructure to tax incentives designed to attract business of all sorts, but particularly those with forward-looking tech interests.

Boston and the World Economic Forum's cooperation and the Swedish government's private testing program underscore a central necessity for government to take full advantage of the opportunities afforded by technology and other drivers of change—but not necessarily on their own. In so many words, evolving models of government should acknowledge that effective governance in the future will mandate partnerships with the private sector and other nongovernmental stakeholders.

It makes sense on any number of levels. For one thing, as is the case with individuals, evolving technology has shifted autonomous influence away from government toward a more cooperative, collaborative environment. Moreover, it's in government's own best interests to partner with and follow the lead of private entities. Given government's history of deliberate adoption of new tools and procedures, it's far better to work closely with others who are far more receptive and responsive to such change. That may go a long way toward preventing the amount of change outpacing government's ability to remain as current as possible, not to mention offering partners from whom government can learn through both example and hands-on, experiential activity.

Lastly, nurturing partnerships between government entities and others reinforces the argument that "going it alone" is fast becoming implausible in a fast-changing world. To meet increasingly complex and challenging issues, government should leverage the knowledge and resources of the private sector to foster better governmental and policy outcomes.

Other examples highlight how increasingly commonplace (and powerful) such partnerships can be. Introduced in 2010, Coca-Cola's 5by20 Initiative works closely with local governments around the world to empower women entrepreneurs.[10] Beer maker Heineken has partnered with the Dutch and Ethiopian governments to source barley locally.[11] India has worked with drug manufacturer Johnson & Johnson to develop a new tuberculosis drug.[12]

But opportunity in government is by no means limited to the working and function of government itself. Given the vast amount of change ongoing in government, citizens as well will be charged with becoming better, more informed, and more involved. These "digital citizens" will be afforded the opportunity to make the most of a more efficient and effective government, provided they have the tools with which to do so and the know-how to use them effectively.

That can begin with educating oneself about the new technology and services inherent in a more tech-savvy government. For instance, a government that offers certain services online can be a wonderful convenience, but only if the citizens it serves know how to use that technology effectively.

GET ME COPYRIGHT, QUICK!

I needed to apply for a copyright for material I created for online courses. I'd often heard that the online website for obtaining US copyrights was a bear to navigate, so I procrastinated for nearly two years before attempting to file because I didn't want to deal with red tape in any form. Then the lockdown happened, and I was stuck in my home with very little to do. I didn't want to look back on all that free time and regret things I didn't do, so I hopped onto the website with conviction. A process I thought would take hours only took about 20 minutes, and that included reading directions on how to properly answer the questions. For a government that's usually mired in red

continued

tape and endless delays, the process was easy and quick. Kudos to whomever created this ease of use. A month later, I received a paper certificate with my copyright information for my records. It was so easy. Now I do everything online. I'm kicking myself for not doing this two years ago!

—S. K., Teacher, San Leandro, CA

Further, citizens must up their game in other areas to be more complete digital members of society. A deeper comprehensive understanding of the new parameters of online privacy and an awareness of the ethics of online behavior are essential if people are to grow into digital citizens who are constructively engaged in the functioning of government and society in general. The goal of greater media literacy in the schools and elsewhere can serve to address these and other relevant needs, not to mention the policy decay cited earlier that more engaged citizenry can help combat.

That is consistent with another opportunity—government's ability to develop and manage policy-making that is much more inclusive and human-centered than it might have been in the past. While that allows for greater citizen input and involvement—yet another counterargument against the fear of utter technological dominance and control—technology allows governments of varied sizes to better manage, analyze, and, perhaps most important, respond quickly and effectively to such participation and input.

This group-focused policy development process is known as Crowd-Law. In essence, CrowdLaw uses technology to leverage the intelligence and expertise of the public in order to improve the quality of lawmaking. Worldwide, there are already more than two dozen examples of local legislatures and national parliaments turning to the internet to involve the public in legislative drafting and decision-making.

Those and other similar measures highlight the opportunity government has to be significantly more inclusive and to involve many more parties and stakeholders in the varied processes of governing. Rather than treating those outside government as mere recipients of policy and regulation, government can proactively involve those people and organizations whose needs and well-being will be impacted by such measures. In addition to soliciting a wide range of opinions and input to arrive at better, more systemically driven decisions, policy creation shifts more toward the end user. That can speed policy development and implementation, as well as potentially avoid policy overreach and needless regulation.

AI FOR ELECTION INTEGRITY

An ongoing item in the news in the post-pandemic world is the "concern" over voter fraud (quotes are used to point out that experts have agreed for years that voter fraud and other forms of purported mischief are almost exclusively imaginary). In light of that, it's refreshing to find that artificial intelligence is being employed in a much more legitimate capacity—effective monitoring and expansion of voter rolls. The brainchild of data scientist Jeff Jonas, the software is known as Electronic Registration Information Center (ERIC). The technology identifies eligible voters and cleans up voter rolls. Since its founding in 2012, the system has identified 26 million people throughout the country who are eligible but unregistered to vote, as well as 10 million registered voters who have relocated, who have died, or whose name is duplicated on more than one list.[13] With regard to unregistered voters, the system then mails notifications to those people alerting them of their eligibility. Not only has ERIC been a boon to solidifying the integrity of elections across the United States, but officials also agree that the program has decidedly boosted voter turnout and participation—the goal of any vibrant democracy.

—Jeff Wuorio

Responding to the need for government to leverage the amount and impact of change, the World Economic Forum in December 2020 produced Agile Regulation for the Fourth Industrial Revolution, a toolkit of strategies and techniques government can use to help respond in a more responsive way to innovation and disruption. It includes case studies from leading regulators on how to apply these ideas in practice, as well as ideas on how to introduce these approaches across the whole of government, from regulation of autonomous vehicles to the fight against climate change and global warming.

One underlying idea behind such programs is that, historically speaking, government has struggled to keep pace with innovation, hindering its ability to provide citizens with the most up-to-date effective policies and regulations possible. That, in turn, highlights a call to action for government—pursue financial funding for technological advances as proactively as possible. Although one such example—the proposal from the Biden administration for $9 billion for the Technology Modernization Fund, a 3,600 percent increase over the $25 million it received in fiscal year 2020—was ultimately dropped, it's indicative of the sort of forward-thinking financial awareness government will have to employ to systematically build, upgrade, and leverage technological advances in their varied forms.[14]

CHAPTER 9—LEARN AND TRANSFORM

1. Although technology of all sorts holds extraordinary promise, the future of government lies in a decidedly less tech, more human form of operation. Whether a greater inclusion of citizens in the creation of policy or technology that affords greater human contact in government when necessary, a more empathetic approach is shifting the overall focus and activity of government to the end user—those impacted by the laws and regulations that are the

purview of government. Ideally, the end result will be better-crafted laws and regulations that prioritize those they will impact.

2. Greater citizen participation lies at the heart of this highly empathetic approach. Governments have the opportunity to make citizen participation more meaningful and immersive by encouraging growing levels of participation. That can occur through greater transparency and information sharing, involvement in community projects and programs, and, ultimately, a hand in developing policy itself. This greater focus on the end user can produce more effective, longer-lasting policy and regulation, as well as a greater sense of citizen satisfaction in government—a mindset that can prove invaluable when it comes to soliciting the population for financial support.

3. This greater sense of overall involvement also carries over into other areas. Increasingly, government can look to partner with the private sector regarding a variety of programs and projects, be it through financial support or simply serving as mentors of sorts to help government gain experiential grounding in varied forms of technology. In an era where divisions are fast crumbling, a "go it alone" approach is no longer sensible or simply viable. The private sector can offer the technological chops to help government get up to speed and stay there.

SECTION THREE

BE TRANSFORMATIONAL

AN AFRICAN PROVERB SAYS, "If you want to go fast, go alone. If you want to go far, go together."

Those words certainly capture the dichotomy we are living in. Change is upon us; it's come very, very quickly and is only going to accelerate in speed. That change has elevated the individual to a newfound level of leadership, empowered with the tools and the environment to communicate, adapt, and impact like never before. This is taking place throughout society, from education to health care to how we work, play, and govern ourselves.

But, like every dichotomy, there's another side to the coin. While change has occurred quickly, its ramifications are likely to remain in place for some time to come. And, as the African axiom puts it, to attain all the opportunity this rapid change has made possible, we're going to have to come together to build lasting, meaningful change. And that sort of unified effort will be served best by implementing and practicing transformational leadership.

As individual leaders in our own right, transformational leadership affords the best opportunity to both manage widespread change and leverage it for the best possible outcome—for all of us to live better, longer, more safely, and with greater fulfillment.

But that will mandate more than good intentions. It will require a sense of connection with others and systemic thinking and execution to realize the full potential of transformational leadership.

Granted, leaders at all levels face intimidating headwinds. For one thing, rather than looking to "get back to normal," we must confront the reality that change has crafted a new reality. From businesses dealing with the new dynamics of their respective marketplaces to society coming to grips with issues such as climate change and pervasive misinformation, precious little remains as it was just a short time ago. Varied playing fields have not merely shifted but also been completely plowed under and resodded in drastically different ways.

Perhaps even more significant, as was pointed out earlier, leaders also have to cope with dipping trust and confidence in leadership itself. A 2020 Gallup poll found that Americans' trust in the federal government to handle domestic issues is near its lowest point since 1972. Just as disturbing, Americans' trust in *each other's* judgment slipped to a tie with its all-time low.[1]

At a time when the country is struggling to combat the medical, economic, and societal devastation of the global pandemic, it seems we don't have a lot of faith in our leaders or even each other.

Put bluntly, that atmosphere of cynicism and mistrust serves as an unmistakable call for a continued change in leadership style. This section will not only make the case for transformational leadership but also offer a road map for leaders—strategies, principles, and action that embody a transformational leader, with particular emphasis on empathy, systemic thinking and execution, and immersive, experiential learning and growth.

Before we get into the specifics of adopting and employing a transformational leadership style, let's quickly revisit what it's all about.

Initially coined by leadership expert and presidential biographer James MacGregor Burns, transformational leadership is geared to fostering an environment characterized by strong, shared motivation and morale. Emphasizing vision and a close connection with whom they work, transformational leaders inspire and motivate those around them to devote themselves to a mutually beneficial outcome or goal. With transformational leadership, people tend to abandon their own personal self-interests in favor of the organization's objectives because they embrace those priorities themselves.

More specifically, transformational leaders emphasize creative, fresh problem-solving rather than relegating themselves and others to a status quo approach to challenges. In a world where problems are coming at us all faster and with greater variety, a leadership that supports outside-the-box thinking is best positioned to adapt and adjust to how we all address issues of concern.

Like the disruptors and forces of change that the world is experiencing, transformational leadership puts the individual at the heart of the matter. Instead of seeing others as subordinates poised to respond to the slightest command, transformational leaders see others more as partners—individuals whose overall well-being and quality of life matter as much as job performance. That's consistent with the rise of the individual across varied lines.

Additionally, transformational leaders are role models. To connect and inspire, they live by the very same values and attributes that they want others to espouse. As the value of "good work" and corporate and organizational values become increasingly embraced, transformational leaders understand the bonding value of a positive example.

Moreover, transformational leadership simply works. A study published in the *Journal of Occupational and Environmental Medicine* surveyed workers at several different German information and communication technology companies about their employers' leadership styles.

A score for transformational leadership was then determined based on factors such as providing intellectual stimulation, offering positive feedback for good performance, leading by example, and urging employees to feel as though they were contributing to the group's goals.

Research determined that employees with transformational leaders had higher reported levels of well-being. Other factors such as age, work stress, and education had little impact on the results.

"The results of this study suggest that a transformational leadership style, which both conveys a sense of trust and meaningfulness and individually challenges and develops employees, also has a positive effect on employee well-being," the authors summarized.[2]

Simply put, transformational leadership makes sense for a world where change is the only constant. Moving away from the old motivations of bureaucratic powers toward inspiring people to believe in a vision of a cause greater than themselves is in line with our changing values, priorities, and attitudes.

But it cannot happen all by itself. As will be examined in greater detail in the next two chapters, a transformational leader needs to be genuinely empathetic. Lacking that conscious connection with others, even the most uplifting of leaders will be sorely challenged to build the sort of bond that boosts commitment, energy, and performance. It simply cannot be faked.

Additionally, transformational leadership needs systemic planning and application to produce a lasting impact. To use a simple example, a leader who traditionally turned to transactional leadership cannot simply "flip a switch" and become transformational—at least in an effective manner. Rather, leaders need to examine their leadership challenges and priorities and determine what components of transformational leadership—be it serving as a role model, greater empowerment, or other strategy—work most effectively in a given situation.

By contrast, a more scattered approach may not only prove unsuccessful but also leave others wondering about the puzzling shift in leadership style. For transformational leadership to be leveraged to the fullest extent possible, a group should understand why transformational leadership principles are being applied, as well as how they may benefit and grow accordingly.

The stakes are decidedly high. Former Cisco CEO John Chambers has said that as many as 40 percent of companies in business today will not exist in 10 years if they don't reinvent the ways in which they operate and how their leaders approach their roles.[3]

We're all in the same boat somewhat. Not to suggest inevitable extinction, but no matter if it's a question of our careers, education, or government, leadership reinvention is imperative to make the most of the opportunities that change affords. Failing that, we all become more vulnerable to the pitfalls that sweeping change creates for those who refuse to act.

So, breaking things down a bit further, what sorts of thinking, practices, and actions compose a transformational leader? An absolutely complete discussion is beyond the purview of this book, but the following chapters will offer an overview of a number of valuable strategies and ideas that we as the leaders we are all becoming can embrace and implement.

The importance of action, and not merely different ways of thinking, cannot be overstated. As the title of this book notes, empathy must be accompanied by thoughtful execution so that the many benefits of transformational leadership can be fully realized.

CHAPTER 10

THE OVERRIDING ESSENTIAL— EMOTIONAL INTELLIGENCE

ALTHOUGH TRANSFORMATIONAL LEADERSHIP incorporates a number of components, if one concept encapsulates many of the varied characteristics, it might well be emotional intelligence.

Emotional intelligence can be described as the capacity to be keenly aware of your own emotions and the impact they can have on any sort of personal or professional relationship.

First coined by researchers at Yale University in the 1990s, emotional intelligence actively engages emotions in decision-making, problem-solving, and other areas—both your emotions and others'.

That sort of empathy is a cornerstone of transformational leadership—and a cornerstone of the leaders that we can all strive to become. So many of the attributes of transformational leadership can be ascribed to this sense of value that emotional intelligence places on how we interact with others.

As has been addressed earlier, emotional intelligence boosts a leader's ability to inspire others. Whether in business, education, politics, or any other area, people are increasingly embracing the importance of a sense of value—that what they're doing is something far beyond a mere paycheck or just something to do, but a goal with inherent, significant meaning.

An emotionally intelligent leader recognizes that need for a greater sense of value. Emotional intelligence helps craft a vision that unites and inspires others. A shared vision moves individuals, as well as various sorts of teams, beyond simple problem-solving and toward a focus on goals beyond the immediate.

THE VALUE OF MEANING

It's startling to recognize how revealing the COVID-19 pandemic has been in terms of human habits and behavior. In one particular setting, I witnessed the persuasion and influence that come from an emotionally connected leadership style—as well as the drawbacks and even the potentially destructive nature of transactional leaders.

For several months, my wife and I volunteered at a COVID-19 vaccination clinic, helping to steer patients through the paperwork involved, as well as the vaccination itself. Prior to each clinic, a person from the health-care provider sponsoring the clinic would give a group briefing, which included nurses, doctors, and lay volunteers such as ourselves.

In one such briefing, the group leader's remarks consisted largely of things he did not want us to do, such as leave coffee cups out in the vaccination area, gather in small groups during slow periods, and other activities that were deemed undesirable. The response of the group was almost palpable. You could feel the energy level drop as the first patients began to come through the door, as though we were all being watched for any possible "violations." The clinic saw a lot of people that day, but the experience was hardly memorable. It seemed as though we were all looking over our shoulders most of the time rather than giving our attention and energy to those receiving vaccinations.

In contrast, another clinic only a week later had a completely different vibe, one that also began with the pre-clinic gathering. There, a different group leader emphasized the greater significance of what we were going to be doing that day—inoculating hundreds of people against a deadly pandemic, one of just several clinics operating in the area that same day. How proud we all should be of ourselves to come together in such an effort, how we were truly making a difference in our community. To a group that had experienced the frustration and helplessness of the prior months of the pandemic, the feeling that we were all beginning to fight back was liberating.

The interesting distinction—other than that from the prior clinic where we were treated like naughty schoolchildren—was that this wasn't just a meaningless pep rally, filled with hollow rah-rah. Instead, these remarks were not only based on fact—we were helping hundreds of our neighbors and friends—but also lent themselves to a higher, more significant goal. We were there for something greater than ourselves, and the sense of mission was very real.

The resulting atmosphere was electric—purposeful, joyful, and perhaps even more efficient than the clinic a week prior. In retrospect, had the first clinic's leader also emphasized those sorts of group values and mission along with mentions of "don't dos," it would certainly have upped the enthusiasm of the gathered group. It truly underscores the difference that emotionally intelligent leadership can make by raising the bar of significance and meaning. And that goes for volunteers, as well as those earning a paycheck. Why you're there isn't a question of money. Why you're there has everything to do with a higher purpose—something that emotionally tuned-in leadership understands and addresses.

—Jeff Wuorio

A key element of emotional intelligence—and, hence, transformational leadership—is a willingness to accept uncertainty. An emotionally intelligent individual recognizes that the world is a volatile place—perhaps now so more than ever. Accordingly, transformational leadership encourages flexibility, creativity, and approaches that are more adaptive to uncertainty. That's a solid strategy, be it in education, government, or business, encouraging buy-in and individual empowerment.

Fig. 10.1. Photo by Canva Studio from Pexels.

It's also a powerful strategy for the individual leader. Research has shown that those who possess emotional intelligence tend to advance in their careers (emotional intelligence is a particularly strong predictor of job performance). Like others who are simply happier through their connection to something of value, an emotionally tuned-in leader also simply tends to be a more content individual—again, consistent with the overall shift toward a greater focus on personal and professional satisfaction. Leaders feel good because they believe in what they're doing. Accordingly, they direct both their thinking and actions toward that greater good.

The issue of uncertainty also relates to the importance of a leader's experiential learning. As most everything in the world changes and continues to change at an exponentially growing rate, many traditional and conventional forms of problem-solving and leadership are simply no longer effective. But that doesn't necessarily make transformational leadership a slam dunk. Rather, it's critical that leaders learn from their use of transformational leadership as they apply it, thereby allowing adjustments on the fly and shifting strategies to determine what components work best. In effect, transformational leaders must learn as they go to pinpoint leadership qualities and skills that produce the best and longest-lasting outcomes.

Another factor in emotional intelligence is trustworthiness. Since the COVID-19 pandemic has forced millions of workers to become self-motivated and self-managing, the importance of trust is crucial for success. It will be incumbent on leaders to be as transparent as possible to maintain overall employee morale and motivation during such periods of disruption.

That also underscores the value of genuine empathy. An emotionally aware leader needs to develop and sustain an emotional connection with others—not merely to gauge how effective their leadership is but also to effectively acknowledge a greater sense of independence and trust in others' growing autonomy. Phrased another way, an empathetic leader is comfortable with others' own leadership abilities and makes certain that others in the group recognize that level of comfort and feel appropriately supported.

A MORE LEVEL PLAYING FIELD

Over my 30-plus years in corporate America, I've held C-level positions with companies both large and small. In the years before I became an executive, I answered to many executives in the typical "transactional" leadership dynamic, and it left me wanting more—a connection, a common goal, or at least some humanity. Once I achieved the level of chief financial officer by the age of 32, I realized that treating my staff the way I'd been treated was (1) not in my nature, (2) contrary to what I knew would motivate them, and (3) an ineffective way to help them grow. The first step I took was to show them I knew how to do all their jobs, which came as a huge shock to them. All they'd ever known were CFOs who barked orders and made ridiculous demands of them. My actions leveled the playing

continued

field and gave my staff the reassurance of knowing that I'd paid my
dues (and mine was a position they could strive for) and that I came
from a place of experience and knowledge. As a result, ours was a
supportive, collaborative team whose members had mutual respect
for one another.

—Shelley Moench-Kelly

So, emotional intelligence works. Moreover, it's geared to change. It
recognizes the presence of flux and adapts accordingly, no matter the setting, others who may be involved, or any desired outcome.

So, can a person just "become" an emotionally connected leader?
That question has been debated by scholars for some time. But it seems
clear that anyone can adopt many of the essential components of emotional intelligence by considering their attitudes, their frame of mind and
actions, and how consistent they may be with the qualities of emotionally
intelligent leadership. Moreover, research suggests these sorts of emotionally intelligent skills can be learned at any age, refuting the potential
concern that "I'm just too old to change who I am."

HARD-NOSED, BUT TRANSFORMATIONAL

My physical education teacher in grade school was a no-nonsense,
gruff old-timer who had little patience for his students. He'd put us
through endless drills come rain or come shine and was quite mer-
ciless if a student got whiny or didn't want to participate. One day, I
fell and sprained my ankle and feared he'd yell at me to finish the drill
with not a care for my pain. Surprisingly, he walked over and knelt
down beside me. "Can you wiggle your toes, lad?" he asked gently. I
could, and did. "Okay, hang on tight!" He swooped me up and carried
me to the nurse's office and stayed with me until my parents picked

me up. This happened in the late 1970s. While he wasn't a company boss, he was our teacher, and it surprised all of us that he was so . . . developed. On the surface he just seemed like a ticked-off, grumpy, waiting-to-retire teacher. Looking back, I realize now that he was one of the first and few examples I've had in my life of a transformational leader. He was tough and demanded respect, but he also had a heart of gold and took care of us all.

—G. B., Stylist, Croydon, South London, UK

Fig. 10.2. Photo from RODNAE Productions from Pexels.

Here are some tips to help develop emotional intelligence:

- Adopt a "beginner's mind." Traditional leaders often like to portray themselves as encyclopedic authorities. Not only is that frequently less than accurate, but it also doesn't lend itself in the least to learning new ways of thinking and acting. Instead, consider "beginner's mind"—a mindset that actively welcomes learning experiences, including those related to the development of emotional intelligence. Moreover, those around you will appreciate the spirit of your attitude, and you'll become a much better, more informed and emotionally connected leader positioned to take constructive action.

- Understand that emotional intelligence can comprise various categories. As indicated earlier in this chapter, empathy is a core component of emotional intelligence. Other elements of emotional sensitivity include the following:

  - Self-awareness. If you don't genuinely know what makes you tick, as well as those things that you find genuinely challenging on an emotional level, it can be awfully difficult to practice empathy and other habits of emotional intelligence. This calls for candid, even brutal self-honesty—not the easiest challenge for many of us to overcome.

  - Motivation. Emotionally intelligent people like what they see inside themselves. That makes motivation a relatively easy characteristic to acquire. If you believe in yourself and appreciate what you're trying to achieve, staying motivated is rarely a problem. The energy will be there.

  - Self-control. It can take a lot for an emotionally intelligent person to fly off the handle. They tend to make fewer impulsive, ill-thought-out decisions and actions. Instead, they give themselves time to think before doing or saying something they may possibly regret later.

○ Social skills. These are emotional intelligence in action. All the emotional intelligence possible can be of little impact if we lack the skills necessary to convey those emotions. (This and other hands-on tips for systemic execution of emotional intelligence will be addressed in chapter 11.)

• Leverage every opportunity to monitor and boost self-awareness. Be forthright when considering your personal weaknesses and drawbacks. Here, techniques such as mindfulness and attention training can prove exceedingly helpful in furthering your self-understanding.

• An additional tip to gaining self-awareness is to begin writing things down—perhaps in a journal or some other sort of ongoing record. For instance, write down, "I am feeling . . ." and, from there, add an honest answer. Pose the same challenges for emotional issues such as anger, frustration, and disappointment. Not only does writing allow you to keep track of your developing self-awareness, but it can also be inherently more thoughtful. You have to take your time more to write down a response, which promotes more careful consideration of your emotions. If possible, give your feeling or reaction a name. That can make the exercise more personal and, as a result, beneficial.

• Try to slow down, particularly in challenging settings. One of the biggest trip-ups to emotional intelligence is, ironically enough, responding emotionally and off the cuff. Take the time to consider any situation and how you can best respond to it. Some people like to practice breathing exercises as a practical strategy to head off the temptation to act needlessly.

• Listen, don't just hear. Transformational leadership's emphasis on empathy involves truly listening to and processing input from others. An emotionally intelligent leader takes the time to acquire and practice effective listening abilities. One way to practice is to listen to a person's comments or remarks, then repeat or paraphrase them as best as you can. This bolsters your ability to pay attention to what you're hearing and to ensure that you're interpreting what you're hearing how the speaker intends it. Additionally, it also assures the person with whom you're speaking that you're making an honest effort to listen to what they have to say—a boost to empathy and connection.

- Another aspect that contributes to emotional intelligence is developing a sense of commonality with others. In many ways, more traditional (translation: less emotionally intelligent) leaders tend toward an "us versus them" mindset. So-and-so is the boss, and all those others are there to do so-and-so's bidding. By contrast, an emotionally intelligent leader feels a part of one large group, with everyone included. This leader recognizes that everyone's actions and feelings impact others and, accordingly, contributes in a positive manner to that synergy.

- If you're prone to knee-jerk, judgmental responses, give some thought to reprogramming that reaction. For example, if your initial thought to a demanding work situation is "Everyone's just out for themselves," consider replacing that with "Everyone wants to do what's best." If you think about it, both statements say essentially the same thing, but with different connotations. Preprogramming yourself to adjust your immediate response to others can lead to greater empathy and mutual understanding.

- Operate from a positive mindset. The example offered in the prior tip illustrates this perfectly. An emotionally aware leader tries to look at situations from a positive standpoint, which can lead to better problem-solving. On the other hand, a leader who inevitably assumes something negative is already placing themselves in an emotional hole that not only is obvious to others but can be tough to dig out of. That can hinder effective problem resolution.

- Consider consequences proactively. Before you do or say something that's going to affect those around you, put yourself in their place first. How would you react to what you're about to say or do? If it's negative, consider other ways of conveying what you want to get across that's more empathetic to its impact on others.

- Take responsibility for your actions. An emotionally tuned-in leader doesn't slough off culpability for something that didn't turn out as planned if they had a direct hand in that outcome. Owning what you do or say is critical to building trust, confidence, and a sense of shared mission. When we succeed, we succeed as a group. If we don't, that's on all of us as well.

- If trying to take on the challenges of developing emotional intelligence seems too daunting, consider seeking out a mentor with emotional intelligence. Someone who possesses the traits of transformational leadership you wish to acquire can prove an immediate, hands-on example of behavior, attitude, and other characteristics. An emotionally astute mentor can also provide valuable feedback and guidance to others looking to develop similar attributes. Alternatively, if you feel you've been successful in developing emotional intelligence, make a point to share what you've learned with others hoping for a similar experience. Asking for their feedback can be valuable in terms of how successful you've been and what you can offer others as a result.

QUESTIONS FOR EMPATHY

Emotional intelligence is an important leadership skill in the workplace. Leaders who are emotionally intelligent are able to open new lines of communication, create understanding, and help achieve common goals. Learning to empathize with your employees and coworkers, and remain calm, can help you to address conflicts early before they escalate.[1]

continued

You don't need to be convinced that empathy is a good thing—not just for ethical reasons but for practical ones, too. While we're still often cautioned to "leave emotions out of it," being able to put yourself in someone else's shoes is a hallmark of emotionally intelligent leadership, not to mention just being a good coworker. It can open up new lines of communication, create understanding, and help everyone achieve common goals.

Of course, none of that means it's easy. There are always going to be times when empathy is uniquely difficult to summon and sustain. When the going gets tough, your patience wears thin, and you can feel your frustration rising, it's enormously difficult to take a deep breath and continue to listen with an open mind. Still, these four empathetic questions I've learned to ask in difficult situations have helped me keep my cool and get to the bottom of whatever the trouble might be.

1. How is this situation affecting you?

No matter how others answer, thank them for sharing their thoughts and let them know you're going to take their point of view seriously. And as you listen to your direct report or colleague's answer, take note of their body language, too. Then encourage the other person to share more specifics about the context or circumstances of their frustration or concern: "You seem upset about this. Could you tell me what initially happened that led to you feeling that way?" Then listen attentively to their feedback so you can try to piece together a causal timeline of events from their own point of view.

2. How is this keeping you from succeeding?

When employees, coworkers, or business partners know they can open up to you about their challenges, it's easier to resolve those conflicts early and avoid losing your patience over a much bigger blowup later. You'll also help build an open work environment that maximizes everyone's talents, rather than one suffused by complaints and paranoia. So if you're feeling irritated by a coworker during a tough predicament, ask what roadblocks are standing in their way. When people feel valued for their contributions, they'll also feel more comfortable explaining—without blame or anger—what's *preventing* them from contributing.

3. What do you think would be the ideal outcome?

Even when an entire team or organization is working toward common ends, individuals still tend to nurture their own goals and aspirations—and that's usually fine! One manager might have an eye on a more advanced leadership position, for example, while a top salesperson may be trying to work toward managing a huge account. When tensions run high, reconnecting with individuals' separate goals can help you tap back into the empathy needed to keep everyone pulling together. Asking your colleagues how and why they would each prefer a certain outcome from the predicament you're all in is a great way to do that.

4. What did you learn from the last big hurdle you cleared?

Job interviewers love to ask this question, and for good reason—it helps them understand at least one obstacle that has stood in the candidate's way and how the candidate worked through it. You can adapt that same question to navigate stressful workplace scenarios, too. It's a great way to keep your own emotions in check while asking somebody to reconnect with their own problem-solving skills.

Rather than wallowing in the hazards of the present situation, you can make room for your coworker or team member to vent a bit—creating an outlet for their anxiety at the same time that you help them recall a template for solving the problem at hand. Here, too, tune into both their verbal and nonverbal cues so you can get a feel for how they've managed adversity in the past—this way you can coax them into readopting the best of those habits and leaving aside the not so productive ones.

Empathetic listeners are quiet and patient—particularly when that's hardest—and they avoid jumping in to fill gaps in the conversation or impose their own assumptions. It takes real effort not to let your own negative feelings overwhelm you in the process, but sometimes the best strategy is the simplest one: Just ask a question.

—Faisal Hoque

CHAPTER 10—LEARN AND TRANSFORM

1. Emotional intelligence lies at the heart of effective transformational leadership. Incorporating trust, a willingness to take risks and to let others do so as well, and other traits compose a style of leadership that's in tune with the ongoing flux of today's world. Moreover, the more things change and evolve, the more the value of emotional intelligence will increase and become increasingly applicable and useful.

2. Empathy is a particularly important emotional component of sensitive, transformative leadership. To elicit the types of behavior and mindset that emotionally intelligent leaders value, it's essential to develop a genuine sense of connection with and understanding of others. A strong group belief in high, meaningful goals and commitment is only possible when a leader truly sees what makes others tick—and what positive actions can be taken to leverage those very personal characteristics.

3. Emotional intelligence doesn't just benefit others. It also works to strengthen your own sense of personal worth, feeling of achievement, and growth. It only makes sense—if everyone around you feels and works better as a result of emotional intelligence qualities, why should you be the exception?

4. Emotional intelligence isn't necessarily something that we're all born with. By approaching the task thoughtfully and systematically, we can all develop the skills and attributes of effective transformative leadership and emotional empathy. To further the effort, try to surround yourself with others who display emotional smarts. We can all certainly learn from one another.

CHAPTER 11

EMOTIONAL INTELLIGENCE, SYSTEMATIC EXECUTION

NOW WE KNOW the components of a transformational leader armed with emotional intelligence. As emerging leaders, we must all understand the varied "soft skills" we need to incorporate into living and working in a world dominated by sweeping change.

It's likely that, prior to the Fourth Industrial Revolution (4IR), employers would have scoffed at soft skills in a business setting, instead writing them off as traits for more creative practitioners, such as writers, artists, therapists, and the like. In this brave new world, however, the need for these skills—as well as the need for a healthy balance between hard and soft skills—is a critical element to success.

Proof of this is an acknowledgment by business leaders over the course of one year as 4IR emerged. In the first report of its kind instigated by Deloitte in 2018, "86 percent of C-level executives said their organizations were doing 'all they could' to create a workforce for Industry 4.0." By the following year, 2019, "fewer than half—47 percent—said the same."[1] While the change is dramatic, it signals a shift in attitudes that in itself represents soft skills: the ability to be vulnerable and acknowledge reality instead of assuming a tough facade of "everything's just fine; we're ready to tackle this!"

As Dr. Seren Dalkiran, a specialist in the workplace of the future, notes in a TED talk, "Now, more than ever, it is our collective calling: Business as usual does not respond to the emerging new reality. We are in transition. We need a new story, a new way to carve out our collective sense of direction in multiple ways. While we are technologically advancing at such a tremendous rate and speed, morally, we are regressing. We need to shift from an 'ego' system to an 'eco' system."[2]

Fig. 11.1. Photo by Alexander Suhorucov from Pexels.

The Saïd Business School at the University of Oxford published *From Ego to Eco: Leadership for the Fourth Industrial Revolution* that delves deeper into the "ego to eco" transformation.[3]

So important is this topic that New York City-based Fordham University's Gabelli School of Business offers a Thoughtful Leadership Certification Program that "is grounded in the Jesuit ethos of cura personalis, or 'care for the whole person.'"[4] The program has been field-tested with enthusiastic reviews by executives from Fortune 500 companies, including Pfizer, Tiffany & Co., Thomson Reuters, and Capital One.

But knowing what composes that sort of leadership is only part of an effective solution. How to execute that leadership to bring about meaningful, lasting change is every bit as important. Phrased another way, it's critical to connect the emotional intelligence inherent in transformational leadership to systematic thinking and action—a pragmatic, disciplined approach to planning and execution that embodies (and delivers) the principles of transformational leadership. That convergence of our emotional selves with an actionable methodology offers the best opportunity to leverage change to build long-term value, not merely short-term answers with little or no lasting relevance.

Fig. 11.2. Photo by fauxels from Pexels.

This is an essential connection to establish. If you've followed some of the suggestions in the prior chapter regarding the development of emotional intelligence, that's an excellent start to crafting leadership skills in tune with the changing nature of how we live. But an optimal mindset is of little value unless it's applied intelligently and consistently. In essence, you need to learn how to systematically execute emotional intelligence to become an effective transformational leader—an enormous opportunity that circumstances have crafted for all of us.

One certainty lies at the heart of successful leadership. No matter if it's business, education, government, or just ourselves, constant reinvention is an absolute must. Managing and leveraging the exponential level of change we're all experiencing mandates ongoing adaptation and flexibility. Customers are changing. Students are changing. Where and how you work and play are changing. Anyone or anything who fails to recognize this or fails to pivot is doomed to struggle.

It starts with constantly asking questions. Trying to anticipate the future is a dicey game, but the more questions we ask, the more we're likely to come upon answers that offer meaningful guideposts to what we need to know and, from there, act upon. Consider this:

- Is what we're (or I'm) doing now really working? Is the current strategy effective, and if so, is its execution the best it can be? Are the methods used for testing current strategy accurate, as well as thorough? Are other means of testing and evaluation available that might prove more useful?

- Will what we do today have long-term ramifications for the future? Building meaningful, long-term change doesn't happen overnight, but today's actions and decisions can contribute systematically to lasting, positive outcomes. Balance a focus on today with a longer horizon. Be mindful of what's happening right now, as well as its relationship to the long term.

- How do others on the "outside" perceive what we're doing? Our own beliefs and opinions can suffer from tunnel vision. Constantly investigate how customers, students, citizens, and others see your activities. Do they support what you are doing? Are you aligned with their changing needs and priorities?

- Do I have what I need to help ensure a successful change or shift? Change may be inevitable, but it's never prudent to rush into anything without considering your resources. Whether it's financial, a matter of new technology, additional training, or even public opinion, do you and anyone else involved have all that's necessary to execute change or pivot successfully? Further, if you lack something, what can you do about it? Have you considered some form of collaboration to acquire any necessary resources or skills?

- What hints can current events offer? This was touched on earlier, but watching the news with an eye toward subtle implications can provide clues about shifting attitudes, values, and opportunities— as well as the tools with which to leverage them most effectively. In a world characterized by change, small matters can quickly become significant and meaningful.

- Are we getting the most out of what information we can access? One of the biggest challenges to reinvention is a tsunami of information—with so much to sort through, is truly valuable information and data slipping through the cracks? Creating "filters" to capture useful information is one way to make the most of what matters. Filters can be put into place with decision-making groups. Consider how information makes its way through your organization—who passes what along to whom and when? Is everyone within that chain authorized (and comfortable) pointing out both possible opportunities and foreseeable problems?

- Are we charting change? Reinvention requires context. It's always helpful to know the detailed course of how you got from one place to the next. To achieve that, create "artifacts"—notes and records of conversations, meetings, and other activities that culminated in a decision. Take note of your mood and others' at the time of the decision—if someone was angry or anxious, for example, that can help explain why a particular choice was made.

- Considering a change? Conduct a premortem. No matter if it's a shift in what you do as an individual leader or within a large organization, a premortem can help you anticipate problems or issues. With a premortem, you imagine that a particular idea or project has failed, then work your way back to the beginning—a sort of proactive postmortem. In so doing, you may spot problems or issues in advance, giving you the opportunity to correct them before they actually occur. Recall the reference to government providing entrepreneurs venues to test ideas outside the purview of existing regulations. Is there a way to craft a similar "safe" spot for experimentation without real-world consequences?

- Emphasize experiential learning. The importance of reinvention to systematically develop into a transformational leader means that we all have to be paying attention. Is my empathy seen as genuine? Are others responding to my leadership in ways I didn't anticipate? What seems to be genuinely effective in obtaining the results we all desire? Experiential learning affords an ongoing opportunity to continue to learn on the fly and pivot accordingly. There's no better way of determining what's right and what could stand to be improved by firsthand experience. Keep your eyes open and apply what you learn.

A LITTLE APPRECIATION

For some, thoughtful leadership is new and unfamiliar. For me, it is second nature. Perhaps it is because I'm a woman, or perhaps it's because I've been marginalized throughout my career and life, but I'm proud to say that my employees and colleagues have never criticized me for being an old-school transactional leader. I've worked for many such people, and I know how devastating and demoralizing it is. There have been many occasions during my career where I thought I'd succumb to a nervous breakdown, and no job, no amount of money or perks is worth your mental, emotional, or physical health. To my mind, the more you share, the more you receive. I've found that most people are happy with recognition and respect—of course, raises don't hurt either—but I can't tell you the number of people I've known over the last 34 years in my career that have lamented, "All I want is for my boss to appreciate me and my work. A little pat on the back or something. Anything." A little goes a long way, and while these touches don't equate to or replace fair compensation or regular raises, they can do a lot to motivate your staff and keep them loyal.

To illustrate that point, I once had a new employee who, when I called her into my office, bowed her head and moved into my space very slowly. I assured her that I just had a quick, simple question about cross-training. She raised her head to look at me in disbelief. I felt so awful because her actions were identical to that of a stray dog that had been abused. I made it a point to explain my management style to her and to reassure her that she had no reason to fear me. It took her a few months to finally settle down and relax, but she succeeded and was one of my best employees ever. I never asked about her past experience, but I know her psyche was severely damaged because of it.

—Shelley Moench-Kelly

Systematic development and execution of the characteristics of transformational leadership are essential, not just to acquire desirable attributes of transformational leadership but also to implement them effectively. Moreover, carefully planned-out steps to transformational leadership afford the best opportunity to achieve goals and objectives that are as long lasting as they are significant over the short term.

But it's more than just asking the right sorts of questions. Here are some additional tips—many of which are more action-oriented than the prior list of advice—to wed the benefits of transformational leadership to systemic action:

- Focus on purpose and outcomes, not activities. Transformational leadership is, at its heart, hands-off in terms of how intimately involved a leader is in others' activities. Phrased in a different way, transformational leaders never micromanage. They prioritize the end result, not so much the nuts and bolts of the journey that got the team there. They also embrace the greater independence and autonomy that transformational leaders allow others in the group as they work toward the best possible outcome.

- Collaborate, don't compete. Transformational leaders embrace collaboration. Once again, it's the outcome that matters, not just the last one standing. Not only does that translate to an overall emphasis on teamwork and support, but it can also involve collaborating or partnering with others who a more transactional leader might see as competitors or rivals.

A valuable distinction to make with regard to the importance of collaboration is how it differs meaningfully from cooperation. Cooperation is more geared to support, such as someone explaining how a particular piece of technology works. Collaboration, on the other hand, is involved on a greater, deeper level, such as two departments working together on a shared goal or exchanging meaningful information. In a sense, the distinction lies in "ownership"—is a project or activity truly shared or is it more a form of support from someone else? Collaboration implies and mandates a greater level of trust and involvement. In fact, looked at through a somewhat skeptical lens, cooperation can also involve a complete absence of activity or involvement—a sort of cooperation by simply staying out of the way. By building meaningful involvement, collaboration can produce superior results simply by having sufficient trust to tap into the resources of many.

- Don't make solutions and "winning" inseparable. Effective outcomes shouldn't have to involve someone or something "losing." Look to results and how people contributed, rather than accepting that someone or something has to somehow come out on the short end of things. Focus on group success.

ON AGAIN, OFF AGAIN

One situation that many if not most of us have encountered is leaders who are sometimes transformational in their style while completely the opposite at other times. One of my first jobs as a newspaper reporter involved an editor who fit this description perfectly. Most of the time, he was detached, distant, and seemingly uninterested in how others in the company reacted to him. But not always. To cover a four-day sporting event that would be produced as a special edition to the newspaper, he assigned experienced sports reporters, as well as one fairly green rookie—myself. By him selecting me instead of several other more eminently qualified writers, it was clear that he wanted to make me feel more a part of the team rather than the new guy. Additionally, after the special section won several awards, he went out of his way to praise every team member who had participated, singling each of us out for our efforts. We all felt that the praise was equal and inclusive—the group had succeeded, not any one person. Unfortunately, the editor wasted little time in relapsing back into his more common habit to disconnect emotionally. I only

continued

wish one of us—me included—had the nerve to say how much we valued working under his very different leadership style. But I don't think anyone did. And that's a shame.

—Jeff Wuorio

- Embrace the crazy—at least to a certain degree. In an era where creativity and unusual thinking are necessary to address increasingly complex problems and issues, it's valuable not to rule anything out. For instance, in a business setting, consider earmarking funding and resources for early-stage investigation of what might seem unreasonable—at first. In education, greater individual student influence will likely mean greater pursuit of outside-the-box topics and ideas. That can help contribute to learning new skills and tasks that may not be defined or even exist yet. Here, systemic thinking and application can play significant roles in developing systems and settings with which unusual and even revolutionary ideas can be tried out, such as the governmental "sandboxes" described earlier that allow evaluation of new technology and products in a safe, controlled environment.

- Embrace diversity. Transformational leaders who support the inclusivity of others also recognize that working closely as a group may not be particularly effective if everyone involved has the same background and experiences. Take systematic steps to ensure all sorts of diversity in group projects and activities, including age differences, a variety of racial backgrounds, and other elements. The greater the diversity, the more varied the input, which can lead to creative action and problem-solving.

- Develop both the flexibility and capacity to pivot quickly. Be ready and willing to adjust when necessary. On one level, this means being prepared and comfortable with the idea of changing strategies or processes if what is in place isn't working or simply can't accommodate changing conditions—another example of leveraged experiential learning. But a willingness to support the unusual doesn't necessarily mean a blank check. Rather, consider what might be described as flexibility with limits. For instance, with regard to support for students who want to pursue different issues or research, reasonable parameters should be put into place—such as a deadline for a paper or report that details results and supports further investigation. Encourage creativity and curiosity, but not without the presence of fair guidelines.

• To adapt quickly, pay attention to small things. Sometimes, when seemingly insignificant or innocent things occur, it can be all too tempting to dismiss them as outliers. An emotionally intelligent, transformational leader isn't so quick to ignore what might prove important. That said, always keep an eye open for early harbingers of significant disruption or change—for instance, feedback from customers that's seemingly growing in strength, citizen interest in a governmental project that's not a priority at the moment, and even a restructuring of leadership where you work. The sooner you can sense change building, the faster and more effectively you can adapt and respond.

• Know what to say and what not to say. Unlike their more trans-actionally minded colleagues, transformational leaders need to be aware of the consequences and implications of what they say to others, even in what seem to be innocent conversations. While recognizing and developing emotional intelligence are vital for survival and growth in today's workplace and in society, so is the ability to identify those who haven't yet reached a heightened level of emotional intelligence. According to Dr. Les Carter, a therapist who has conducted more than 60,000 counseling sessions, there are 12 phrases that emotionally intelligent people do not use.[5] At first, they all might seem like neutral, interactive components of a conversation, but looking deeper at their true meanings reveals "covert" or passive-aggressive attitudes that aren't clearly evident at first glance. In fact, they subversively place blame on the listener:

- You're going to do what?

- Okay, if that's what you want to think.

- I had no other choice.

- How do you think I'm supposed to feel?

- If you can believe that . . .

- Everything is great, right?

- Well, aren't you just being sensitive?

- Nobody says that to me . . .

- This would never have happened if you had . . .

- Stop it! Just stop it!

- That reminds me of a time when I . . .

- Why should I even bother with you?

- **Be an exponential leader.** It seems clear that an effective transformational leader will have to wear many hats, some of which they may never have even dreamed of trying on. But that's really no different from so much of the change and disruption we've experienced and will continue to witness—new ways of thinking, new skills, and new approaches. That in turn argues for the value of a transformational leader who is also an exponential leader—one who is willing to acquire and apply a variety of different skills and approaches, including these:

- ○ Futurist—You're not afraid to think of bold, new ideas.

- ○ Humanitarian—You make choices geared to making a positive impact on others and your community.

- ○ Innovator—You're able to move ideas into actual reality.

- ○ Technologist—You leverage technology to better results in all sorts of ways.

- Understand what the true long-term objective is. A famous quote often attributed to Tom Peters (and others) holds that "leaders don't create followers; they create more leaders." This, as much as anything else, captures the essence of transformational leadership in action—particularly in a world geared to opportunity for leadership at all levels of society. Compliance is not the goal. Skilled, connected, and practical leadership are.

NO FEAR

I'm close to retirement, maybe in the next three years. Five years ago, my boss retired and was replaced with this young man who was younger than my youngest child. I knew more about my industry in my little finger than he knew in his entire life, and I didn't initially like him. He was a little too much "How does that make you feel?" and I thought he was insane. All I knew was performance, not feelings. He wore me down, though. It took about six months. One day I just snapped because I didn't know what he was aiming for with all this talk about feelings. I felt like he was trying to dig up some dirt on me, like a psychologist or something, maybe even a company "plant." He was so calm and explained his leadership style, which isn't one I've ever heard of. I've gotta say, this kid has helped me grow as an employee and as a human being. He's not one of the "bad guys" who are only out to make money off my blood, sweat, and tears. Once we understood each other, I wasn't as defensive, and my overall

continued

feeling about work went from tolerating it to actually enjoying it. And yes, I admit that openly, because I learned from him that it's okay to express yourself without fear of retribution.

—R. G., Translator, Spokane, WA

These and other strategies for execution and reinvention lend discipline to the pursuit of creativity, flexibility, and innovation—hallmarks of a changing world. In a way, it's very much a reciprocal relationship. An open and adaptive leadership style is designed to foster inspiration and resourcefulness, and it is balanced by a systematic and pragmatic system of organization and execution—security working in harmony with volatility and flux.

THE IMPERATIVE OF DESIGN THINKING

In today's rapidly developing and increasingly digital world, organizations face many challenges. These include disruptive technologies, economic and political pressures, and keeping up with changes in customer behavior.

What happens when businesses fumble or turn a blind eye to change? Take ESPN as an example.[6] A 2017 *New York Times* article noted, "The 'Worldwide Leader in Sports,' as ESPN branded itself, laid off scores of journalists and on-air talent on Wednesday, showing that even the most formidable media kingdom was vulnerable to the transformation upending the sports broadcasting industry as more and more people turn away from cable television."[7]

The network has lost over 10 million viewers over the past few years. Disney, ESPN's major shareholder, planned to revive ESPN's growth via subscription streaming services—a digital transformation strategy to keep up with changing consumer behavior.

The New York Times reports that the streaming service offering will leverage Disney's purchase of BamTech and will allow streaming of hockey, tennis, cricket, and college sports.

Robert Iger, former Disney CEO, had this to say: "You have to be willing to either create or experience some distribution as we migrate from what has been a more traditionally distributed world to a more nontraditional distribution world. And some of that we're going to end up doing to ourselves, meaning that we understand there is disruption, but we believe we have to be a disrupter too."[8]

We are inundated by a new wave of challenges and opportunities as the planet becomes increasingly connected.

Today technologies have wildly different fates:[9]

- Anything that can be digitized will be.
- Anything that can go wireless will.
- Anything that can get smaller will.
- And information will move more freely.

Technological or digital transformations will continue to reshape the way the business world is organized. As information becomes more plentiful and less centralized, more organizations are likely to decentralize too, in order to respond swiftly to it all.

However, a recent leadership study on digital transformation by Dell unveils most organizations are unprepared:[10]

- A full 45 percent fear becoming obsolete in three to five years.
- A full 48 percent are unaware of what their industry will look like in three years.
- Only 5 percent are classified as Digital Leaders.

Digital transformation can be defined as a process whereby an organization shifts their business models, processes, and organizational culture with digital technologies to adapt to changing customer behaviors. They adapt to meet ever-changing customer expectations and engage with consumers in innovative ways.[11]

Today, products and services are entering the marketplace more quickly than ever before, and product life cycles are shrinking. Now, customers demand simplicity, flexibility, and speed. Therefore, technology has become an essential tool in fulfilling their needs and providing positive experiences. Organizations must keep up,

continued

innovate, and use digital solutions to retain and build stronger customer relationships, as well as generate new revenue streams.

Steve Jobs once said, "Most people make the mistake of thinking design is what it looks like. People think it's this veneer—that the designers are handed this box and told, 'Make it look good!' That's not what we think design is. It's not just what it looks like and feels like. Design is how it works."[12]

For decades, analytical thinking was the standard approach used to solve client-facing problems. However, with all the challenges and opportunities brought about by an increasingly technically advanced world, our approach for problem-solving has to change as well. This is where "design thinking" can make a substantial difference.

A recent *Fast Company* article defines design thinking: "Although Design is most often used to describe an object or end result, Design in its most effective form is a process, an action, a verb not a noun. A protocol for solving problems and discovering new opportunities. Techniques and tools differ and their effectiveness are arguable but the core of the process stays the same. It's taken years of slogging through Design = high style to bring us full circle to the simple truth about design thinking. That it is a most powerful tool and when used effectively, can be the foundation for driving a brand or business forward."[13]

Over the years, this is what I have learned about design thinking and how it can move any organization forward.[14]

***First*, adapt a basic framework.** Contrary to the popular belief that design thinking is only used for a new product or service, it is the existing business processes that greatly benefit from design thinking, as they are what usually needs to be reinvented the most.

Although there are many models and frameworks available for applying design thinking, let's establish some basic concepts:

1. **Research**—Do extensive cross-industry market research, both qualitative and quantitative, to understand current and changing customer behavior.
2. **Define**—Define the problem that needs solving.
3. **Ideate**—Consider many options from many perspectives, disciplines, and sources. Design thinking requires multiple

iterations of idea generation before picking the ultimate winning idea.

4. **Execute**—Develop rapid prototypes to gather feedback from stakeholders. Once the final solution is refined and approved, an execution plan is then produced to move forward.

Design thinking is not just about creativity, as complex problem-solving also requires a collaborative approach, incorporating all parts of an organization—from internal resources to partners and customers.

Second, **build agile and adaptive organizations.** Organizations that can successfully navigate digital disruptions need to then put that agile mindset into practice. Agility, by definition, is a business's response to changes—whether those come from new macro- or microeconomic conditions; after all, some disruption snowballs from something that starts small, and other times it arises from massive pressures.

Such organizations are characterized by flexibility and are able to keep up with the changes that occur in a dynamic marketplace. The synergy between design thinking and agile and adaptable organizations is obvious: The iterative nature of design thinking is such that it allows relevant information to influence eventual product or service design. Similarly, adaptive and agile organizations allow relevant information to shape how they work. When design thinking permeates an agile organization, its efficiency and productivity factors are magnified. Therefore, it makes sense that organizations that adopt design thinking must be agile and adaptable, as they are mutually reinforcing.

Third, **discover new technologies.** Design thinking begins with a discovery process. Understanding how customers are changing is the anchor of digital transformation and design thinking. Today, big data, artificial intelligence (AI), and the Internet of Things (IoT) provide the information that kickstarts the design-thinking process. For example, the IoT phenomenon provides immeasurable insight into the customer's mind by analyzing daily activities. It was predicted that the IoT market would be more than $50 billion by 2020. Technologies are the enablers, causes, and accelerators of digital transformation and the starting point of design thinking.

continued

Digital transformation is centered on enhancing the customer experience. Organizations need to understand their customer's unmet needs. Today, organizations can use analytics and AI to churn the information gathered from big data and the IoT into patterns that reveal what their customers want. It takes the guesswork out of understanding customers and allows brands to align with the values of its customers.

The design-thinking process is a structured yet creative way to facilitate data-driven rapid innovation. It feeds off a cycle of rapid testing of ideas and getting fast feedback from customers to test the validity of concepts. Through rapid testing of ideas, it's easier to separate the good from the crazy from the crazy good. Once an idea is found that can be brought to fruition, it can be formalized, developed, tested, and released. And customer feedback on the final product provides new food for thought that can be used in further innovations.

Therefore, design thinking is well suited for digital transformation. It embraces the need for data-driven innovation and recognizes that no disruptive innovations can be made without understanding the customer's needs.

—Faisal Hoque

CHAPTER 11—LEARN AND TRANSFORM

1. When working to bolster the effectiveness of transformational leadership, pay particular attention to the words and phrases you commonly use with others. As the sample list earlier in this chapter demonstrates, even seemingly innocent remarks can prove to be anything but supportive and empathetic. Generally speaking, phrases that tend to put others on the defensive run counter to the broader goals of transformative leadership. Keep a keen eye out for them and avoid them whenever possible.

2. A transformational leader embraces experiential learning. By focusing on policies, practices, and outcomes, a transformational leader is constantly evaluating what's effective in actual practice. From there, a comfort level with adjustments allows the leader to make adjustments accordingly. A transformational leader also recognizes the novelty of many of the leadership challenges change has introduced in all areas of how we work and play. Since the playbook has yet to be written, learning as you go is the only effective way to navigate leadership challenges effectively.

3. Transformational leaders also encourage meaningful collaboration, not just cooperation. Cooperation by its nature is more limited. Cooperation can also be passive, such as in situations where people "go along" even though they don't truly believe in what is happening. Collaboration, on the other hand, is more involved and more active. It connotes sharing and exchange of resources, skills, and other forms of support. A collaborative environment— one bolstered by common goals, values, and a commitment to success involving all—stands a better chance of fostering lasting, meaningful impact and change than does mere cooperation.

FINAL THOUGHTS

THE MORE THINGS CHANGE, the more they stay the same.

However applicable in many situations, that old adage isn't entirely true when it comes to the level and scope of change that the world is experiencing. With four largely unprecedented drivers—the Fourth Industrial Revolution, COVID-19, climate change, and misinformation—completely upending the ways we live, work, and play, the future poses challenges and opportunities utterly unlike anything the world has seen before.

As has been examined throughout the course of this book, that mandates a decidedly different, more evolved form of leadership—transformational leadership—where we are all more empowered to choose just how we pursue different goals, where collaboration is far more effective and meaningful than the quid pro quo leadership of the past, and where individuals can benefit from unprecedented autonomy and capacity to craft their own lives.

And, as has also been emphasized, that means that we as individuals are now far more imbued with leadership opportunities than ever before. Be it in health-care decisions, how we choose to learn, or how we develop and govern society, we are all positioned to be that much more involved in choices and decisions that not very long ago were out of our hands. That makes transformational leadership a powerful and accessible tool for us all.

And, in what might seem contrary to much of what has been discussed, that will also mandate as systemic an execution of these newfound leadership opportunities as possible. Abstract ideas and concepts can be noble pursuits, but only if there are processes in place to put them into effective practice. Transformational leadership de-emphasizes process in favor of results and outcomes, but implementing the characteristics and practices of transformational leadership mandates practical, empirical application. It's a matter of wedding thought with boots-on-the-ground action.

Further, it's important to recognize several caveats. First is the essential value of experiential learning. Phrased simply, we're going to have to learn and become better at managing and leveraging change as we go—our user's manual is being written on the fly. Real-life observation and evaluation will be key to recognizing what practical strategies work and which ones simply do not. We will all have to live and learn from change in the heart of the experience itself.

Additionally, there is no magic bullet here. No single approach to making the most of the opportunity of the change we have experienced—and will continue to experience—will prove the be-all and end-all solution to the challenges that change poses for us. Rather, it will be a confluence of ideas, strategies, and actions that will prove effective in managing and making the most of sweeping change. That will involve not only constant experiential learning but also a willingness to experiment and improvise. The world that existed yesterday will be decidedly different from that of tomorrow and the day after. It will take a complete and adaptable toolkit for each of us to cope effectively with that ongoing cycle of reinvention.

But it's also an optimistic time to be alive. However grim reality can often be, mistakes, miscalculations, and even the most significant challenges are as mortal as we are. Approach them with the skills and an attitude born of opportunity and possibility, and the future can make the struggles and frustrations of the past seem like distant memories.

ACKNOWLEDGMENTS

INSPIRATION FOR *Lift* stemmed from living through the tsunami of changes and disruptions our world has experienced in recent years. Research into collective global experiences has formed the foundation of this book. My acknowledgment begins with those global citizens who continuously show us the art and science of moving forward.

My publicist, Lori Ames, has been a never-ending support for more than a decade. She is the one who brought together all the connections needed to successfully complete a major project such as this. I am indebted to my content team for their tireless efforts in researching and flowing content with brilliant craftsmanship. Without them, there would be no *Lift*.

Thanks to the entire design, editorial, production, and project management team members at Greenleaf and *Fast Company* that have made *Lift* a reality. Their collective expertise is nothing less than world-class.

My utmost respect goes out to my global teams, partners, and customers for allowing me to be part of their professional lives for so many years. They have allowed me to learn, serve, and grow. I am honored.

I am grateful to my family (near and far) for their unlimited love and support, and there are not enough words for my friends, who are there for me every day.

I am fortunate to have a life partner—my anchor—whose impact is beyond any measure, and a son who is the greatest source of my inspiration. Thanks to my mother for teaching me resilience.

No one survives in a vacuum. My gratitude extends to those who make our lives easier and help us survive when we need them most. The Universe has allowed me to have an amazing life, and for that, I consider myself lucky indeed.

Authors write for readers. Most of all, thank you for reading *Lift*.

—**Faisal Hoque**, October 27, 2021

NOTES

Introduction

1. Schwab, Klaus, *The Fourth Industrial Revolution* (New York: Currency, 2017).
2. Persily, Nathaniel, *The Internet's Challenge to Democracy: Framing the Problem and Assessing Reforms* (Kofi Annan Foundation, 2019), https://pacscenter.stanford.edu/publication/the-internets-challenge-to-democracy-framing-the-problem-and-assessing-reforms/

Chapter 1

1. Lin, Ying, "10 Artificial Intelligence Statistics You Need to Know in 2021," Oberlo, August 22, 2020, https://www.oberlo.com/blog/artificial-intelligence-statistics
2. Thomas, Mike, "29 Top Internet of Things Examples You Should Know," Built In, August 11, 2021, https://builtin.com/internet-things/iot-examples
3. Szymkowski, Sean, "Domino's Pizzas Now Delivered with Autonomous Cars in Houston," CNET, April 12, 2021, https://www.cnet.com/roadshow/news/dominos-pizza-delivery-autonomous-cars-nuro-houston/
4. Associated Press, "Baidu Launches Driverless Taxi Service in Beijing," MarketWatch, May 2, 2021, https://www.marketwatch.com/story/baidu-launches-driverless-taxi-service-in-beijing-01619996028
5. World Economic Forum, *The Future of Jobs*, January 2016, https://www3.weforum.org/docs/WEF_Future_of_Jobs.pdf
6. Hoque, Faisal, "The Case for Humanities in the Era of AI, Automation and Technology," *Fast Company*, September 18, 2018, https://www.fastcompany.com/90236240/the-case-for-humanities-in-the-era-of-ai-automation-and-technology

7. RBC, *Humans Wanted—How Canadian Youth Can Thrive in the Age of Disruption*, March 2018, https://www.rbc.com/dms/enterprise/futurelaunch/_assets-custom/pdf/RBC-Future-Skills-Report-FINAL-Singles.pdf

8. Anders, George, *You Can Do Anything: The Surprising Power of a "Useless" Liberal Arts Education* (New York: Little, Brown, 2017).

9. "Gartner HR Survey Reveals 88 Percent of Organizations Have Encouraged or Required Employees to Work From Home During Coronavirus," Gartner, March 19, 2020, https://www.gartner.com/en/newsroom/press-releases/2020-03-19-gartner-hr-survey-reveals-88--of-organizations-have-e

10. Cole, Jeffrey, "The Two Kinds of Workers after COVID," Center for the Digital Future, October 13, 2021, https://www.digitalcenter.org/columns/two-types-of-workers/

11. Gourarie, Chava, "Spotify Will Allow Its Staff to Work from Anywhere Permanently," *Commercial Observer*, February 12, 2021, https://commercialobserver.com/2021/02/spotify-will-allow-its-staff-to-work-from-anywhere-permanently

12. Maurer, Roy, "Study Finds Productivity Not Deterred by Shift to Remote Work," SHRM, September 16, 2020, https://www.shrm.org/hr-today/news/hr-news/pages/study-productivity-shift-remote-work-covid-coronavirus.aspx

13. Hughes, Owen, "Actually, Remote Working May Not Be the 'New Normal' After All," TechRepublic, March 25, 2021, https://www.techrepublic.com/article/remote-working-may-not-be-the-new-normal-after-all/

14. Spajic, Damjan Jugovic, "The Future of Employment—30 Telling Gig Economy Statistics," Smallbizgenius, May 26, 2021, https://www.smallbizgenius.net/by-the-numbers/gig-economy-statistics/

15. Martin, Nicole, "Artificial Intelligence Is Being Used to Diagnose Disease and Design New Drugs," *Forbes*, September 20, 2019, https://www.forbes.com/sites/nicolemartin1/2019/09/30/artificial-intelligence-is-being-used-to-diagnose-disease-and-design-new-drugs/

16. Penprase, Bryan Edward, "The Fourth Industrial Revolution and Higher Education," in *Higher Education in the Era of the Fourth Industrial Revolution*, ed. Nancy W. Gleason (Singapore: Palgrave Macmillan, 2018), pp. 207–29.

17. France-Presse, Agence, "Smile-to-Pay: Chinese Shoppers Turn to Facial Payment Technology," *The Guardian*, September 4, 2019, https://www.theguardian.com/world/2019/sep/04/smile-to-pay-chinese-shoppers-turn-to-facial-payment-technology

18. Charm, Tamara, et al., "The Great Consumer Shift," McKinsey, August 4, 2020, https://www.mckinsey.com/business-functions/marketing-and-sales/our-insights/the-great-consumer-shift-ten-charts-that-show-how-us-shopping-behavior-is-changing

19. Ditteriech, Thomas G., "Benefits and Risks of Artificial Intelligence," *Medium*, January 22, 2015, https://medium.com/@tdietterich/benefits-and-risks-of-artificial-intelligence-460d288cccf3

20. Pillsbury, Steve, "Why 4IR Is a Love It or Loathe It Proposition," *Digital Pulse*, PwC, November 18, 2019, https://www.pwc.com.au/digitalpulse/4ir-survey-pros-and-cons.html

21. Edsall, Thomas, "Why Trump Still Has Millions of Americans in His Grip," *The New York Times*, May 5, 2021, https://www.nytimes.com/2021/05/05/opinion/trump-automation-artificial-intelligence.html

22. Edsall, Thomas, "Why Trump Still Has Millions of Americans in His Grip," *The New York Times*, May 5, 2021, https://www.nytimes.com/2021/05/05/opinion/trump-automation-artificial-intelligence.html

Chapter 2

1. Sacks, Jonathan, "Rabbi Sacks on the Coronavirus Pandemic," interview by Emily Maitlis, Jonathan Sacks (website), March 19, 2020, https://rabbisacks.org/rabbi-sacks-on-the-coronavirus-pandemic-extended-newsnight-interview/

2. DeSilver, Drew, "Before the Coronavirus, Telework Was an Optional Benefit, Mostly for the Affluent Few," Pew Research Center, March 20, 2020, https://www.pewresearch.org/fact-tank/2020/03/20/before-the-coronavirus-telework-was-an-optional-benefit-mostly-for-the-affluent-few/

3. "Gartner Survey Reveals 82% of Company Leaders Plan to Allow Employees to Work Remotely Some of the Time," Gartner, July 14, 2020, https://www.gartner.com/en/newsroom/press-releases/2020-07-14-gartner-survey-reveals-82-percent-of-company-leaders-plan-to-allow-employees-to-work-remotely-some-of-the-time

4. Hoque, Faisal, "The Paradoxical Traits of Resilient People," *Fast Company*, November 13, 2013, https://www.fastcompany.com/3021513/the-paradoxical-traits-of-resilient-people

5. Pausch, Randy, and Jeffrey Zaslow, *The Last Lecture* (New York: Hyperion, 2008).

6. May, Rollo, *The Courage to Create* (New York: W.W. Norton, 1994).

7. Quote Investigator, citing a 1934 interview with Nicholas Tesla, https://quoteinvestigator.com/2021/10/06/invent-alone/

8. "Why Being a Loner May Be Good for Your Health," BBC Future, 2018, |https://www.bbc.com/future/article/20180228-there-are-benefits-to-being-antisocial-or-a-loner

9. Tzu, Lao, *Tao te Ching*.

10. "Adm. McRaven Urges Graduates to Find Courage to Change the World," UT News, University of Texas at Austin, May 16, 2014, https://news.utexas.edu/2014/05/16/mcraven-urges-graduates-to-find-courage-to-change-the-world/

11. "Adm. McRaven Urges Graduates to Find Courage to Change the World," UT News, University of Texas at Austin, May 16, 2014, https://news.utexas.edu/2014/05/16/mcraven-urges-graduates-to-find-courage-to-change-the-world/

12. Cooper, Taikein, "COVID-19 is Our 'Sputnik' Moment in Education," The 74, February 23, 2021, https://www.the74million.org/article/covid-19-is-our-sputnik-moment-in-education/

13. Jaschik, Scott, "Rowan Offers Incentives to Get Vaccinated," Inside Higher Ed, May 7, 2021, https://www.insidehighered.com/news/2021/11/01/live-updates-latest-news-covid-19-and-higher-education

14. Lieberman, Mark, "5 Things You Need to Know about Student Absences during COVID-19," Education Week, October 16, 2020, https://www.edweek.org/leadership/5-things-you-need-to-know-about-student-absences-during-covid-19/2020/10

15. Chandra, S., et al., Closing the K–12 Digital Divide in the Age of Distance Learning (San Francisco, CA: Common Sense Media; Boston, MA: Boston Consulting Group, 2020).

16. "Consumer Sentiment and Behavior Continue to Reflect the Uncertainty of the COVID-19 Crisis," McKinsey and Company, October 26, 2020, https://www.mckinsey.com/business-functions/marketing-and-sales/our-insights/a-global-view-of-how-consumer-behavior-is-changing-amid-covid-19

17. Skare, Marinko, et al., "Impact of COVID-19 on the Travel and Tourism Industry," Technological Forecasting and Social Change 163 (February 2021).

18. Le Quéré, C., et al., "Temporary Reduction in Daily Global CO_2 Emissions during the COVID-19 Forced Confinement," Nature Climate Change 10 (2020).

Chapter 3

1. World Economic Forum, The Global Risks Report, 16th Edition, 2021, https://www3.weforum.org/docs/WEF_The_Global_Risks_Report_2021.pdf

2. "The Economics of Climate Change," Swiss Re Institute, April 22, 2021, https://www.swissre.com/institute/research/topics-and-risk-dialogues/climate-and-natural-catastrophe-risk/expertise-publication-economics-of-climate-change.html

3. The Changing Atmosphere: Implications for Global Security conference, first paragraph of Conference Statement, 1988.

4. "2019 Was 2nd-Hottest Year on Record for Earth Say NOAA, NASA," National Oceanic and Atmospheric Administration, January 15, 2020, https://www.noaa.gov/news/2019-was-2nd-hottest-year-on-record-for-earth-say-noaa-nasa

5. "Economic Losses from Natural Disasters Top $232 Billion in 2019 as the Costliest Decade on Record Comes to a Close," Aon, January 22, 2020, https://aon.mediaroom.com/2020-01-22-Economic-losses-from-natural-disasters-top-232-billion-in-2019-as-the-costliest-decade-on-record-comes-to-a-close-Aon-catastrophe-report

6. Schlanger, Zoë, "What to Save? Climate Change Forces Brutal Choices at National Parks," *The New York Times*, May 18, 2021, https://www.nytimes.com/2021/05/18/climate/national-parks-climate-change.html

7. Gaarder, Nancy, "Saharan Dust Reaches Omaha Area, Making Air Unhealthy for Some," *Omaha World Herald*, June 29, 2020, https://omaha.com/weather/saharan-dust-reaches-omaha-area-making-air-unhealthy-for-some/article_d62fde09-634a-5096-ab52-1f45b3d7e378.html

8. Women's Forum for the Economy and Society, *Women Leading Climate Action: A World within Reach*, 2019, https://www.womens-forum.com/wp-content/uploads/2020/06/Women4ClimateAction-report_2019.pdf

9. Anderson, Allison, "Building Resilience in Education to the Impact of Climate Change," Brookings Institution, September 17, 2019, https://www.brookings.edu/blog/education-plus-development/2019/09/17/building-resilience-in-education-to-the-impact-of-climate-change/

10. Sakib, Najmus SM, "Climate Crisis Taking Heavy Toll on People of Bangladesh," Anadolu Agency, October 6, 2021, https://www.aa.com.tr/en/asia-pacific/climate-crisis-taking-heavy-toll-on-people-of-bangladesh/2269366

11. Lowenkrom, Hadriana, "Bangladesh Offers a Model for Climate Migration," *Bloomberg*, June 17, 2021, https://www.bloomberg.com/news/articles/2021-06-18/bangladesh-offers-a-model-for-climate-migration

12. "Global Warming to Increase Violent Crime in the United States," CIRES, January 15, 2020, https://cires.colorado.edu/news/global-warming-increase-violent-crime-united-states

13. Burke, Marshall, Solomon Hsiang, and Edward Miguel, "Quantifying the Influence of Climate on Human Conflict," *Science* 341, no 6151 (September 2013).

14. Cilluffo, Anthony, and Neil Ruiz, "World's Population Is Projected to Nearly Stop Growing by the End of the Century," Pew Research Center, June 17, 2019, https://www.pewresearch.org/fact-tank/2019/06/17/worlds-population-is-projected-to-nearly-stop-growing-by-the-end-of-the-century/

15. Mortillaro, Nicole, "Is Population Control the Answer to Fixing Climate Change?" CBC News, October 25, 2019, https://www.cbc.ca/news/science/population-climate-change-1.5331133

16. Alderman, Liz, and Constant Méheut, "Going Green, or Greenwashing? A Proposed Climate Law Divides France," *The New York Times*, May 19, 2021, https://www.nytimes.com/2021/05/19/business/macron-france-climate-bill.html

17. Krosnick, John A., and Bo MacInnis, *Climate Insights 2020, Surveying American Public Opinion on Climate Change and the Environment* (Washington, DC: Resources for the Future, 2020), https://media.rff.org/documents/Climate_Insights_Overall_Trends_Final_RCFAejQ.pdf

18. Schaub, Sarah, "Global Warming: The Predicament, Contributions and Initiatives" (Seminar Paper), April 19, 2012, http://www.philau.edu/collegestudies/Documents/SarahSchaub.pdf

19. Tyson, Alec, and Brian Kennedy, "Two-Thirds of Americans Think Government Should Do More on Climate," Pew Research Center, June 23, 2020, https://www.pewresearch.org/science/2020/06/23/two-thirds-of-americans-think-government-should-do-more-on-climate/

Chapter 4

1. Bremmer, Charles, "Websites Pump Out Fake News Minutes after Offshore Claims," *The Times*, May 5, 2017, https://www.thetimes.co.uk/article/websites-pump-out-fake-news-minutes-after-macron-offshore-claims-7dz366fnl

2. Islam, Saiful et al. "COVID-19–Related Infodemic and Its Impact on Public Health: A Global Social Media Analysis," *American Journal of Tropical Medicine and Hygiene* 103, no. 4 (August 2020).

3. Funke, Daniel, "Study: Fake News Is Making College Students Question All News," Poynter Institute, October 16, 2018, https://www.poynter.org/fact-checking/2018/study-fake-news-is-making-college-students-question-all-news/

4. Baker, Gerard, "Media Mistrust Won't Inoculate You against Misinformation," *Wall Street Journal*, May 3, 2021, https://www.wsj.com/articles/media-mistrust-wont-inoculate-you-against-misinformation-11620061429

5. Hoque, Faisal, "Don't Let Social Media Ruin Your Life and Career," HackerNoon, *Medium*, https://medium.com/hackernoon/dont-let-social-media-ruin-your-life-and-career-6258781971e2

6. Mandell, Andrea, "Disney Fires 'Guardians' Director James Gunn after Tweets about Rape, Pedophilia Unearthed," *USA Today*, July 20, 2018.

7. Gunn, James, "Anyway, that's the completely honest truth," @James Gunn, Twitter, July 19, 2018, 11:53 p.m., https://twitter.com/jamesgunn/status/1020154780012834816?lang=en

8. George, Bill, "Former CEO of Large Multinational: Trump's Trade War Will Raise Prices for Consumers and Could Trigger a Recession," CNBC, July 23, 2018, https://www.cnbc.com/2018/07/23/bill-george-if-trump-follows-through-on-tariffs-consumers-will-pay.html

9. Zeller, Tom, Jr., "Lest We Regret Our Digital Bread Crumbs," *The New York Times*, June 12, 2006, https://www.nytimes.com/2006/06/12/technology/12link.html

10. Allcott, Hunt, and Matthew Gentzkow, "Social Media and Fake News in the 2016 Election," *Journal of Economic Perspectives* 31, no. 2 (Spring 2017).

11. Jamieson, Kathleen Hall, and Daniel Romer, "Conspiracy Theories as Barriers to Controlling the Spread of COVID-19 in the US," *Social Science and Medicine* 263 (October 2020).

12. Schaeffer, Katherine, "A Look at the Americans Who Believe There Is Some Truth to the Conspiracy Theory That COVID-19 Was Planned," Pew Research Center, July 24, 2020, https://www.pewresearch.org/fact-tank/2020/07/24/a-look-at-the-americans-who-believe-there-is-some-truth-to-the-conspiracy-theory-that-covid-19-was-planned/

13. "Onion: 'We Just Fooled the Chinese Government!'" CNN, November 28, 2012, https://www.cnn.com/2012/11/27/world/asia/north-korea-china-onion/index.html

14. Debter, Lauren, "Fitbit Shares Jolted on Suspicious Takeover Bid," *Forbes*, November 10, 2016, https://www.forbes.com/sites/laurengensler/2016/11/10/fitbit-takeover-bid/.

15. "AP FACT CHECK: Coca-Cola Not Recalling Dasani Water," Associated Press, January 24, 2017, https://apnews.com/article/ecfb398fa555456d99fe40e0a05dd1da

16. CHEQ and University of Baltimore, *The Economic Cost of Bad Actors on the Internet*, 2019, https://s3.amazonaws.com/media.mediapost.com/uploads/EconomicCostOfFakeNews.pdf

17. Nyhan, Brendan, "Why the 'Death Panel' Myth Wouldn't Die: Misinformation in the Health Care Reform Debate," *The Forum* 8, no. 1 (January 2010).

18. "Health Care Reform Closely Followed, Much Discussed," Pew Research Center, August 2009, https://www.pewresearch.org/politics/2009/08/20/health-care-reform-closely-followed-much-discussed/.

19. Gupta, Aditi et al., "Faking Sandy: Characterizing and Identifying Fake Images on Twitter during Hurricane Sandy," Proceedings of the 22nd International Conference on World Wide Web, May 2013.

20. Donald, Brooke, "Stanford Researchers Find Students Have Trouble Judging the Credibility of Information Online," Stanford Graduate School of Education, November 22, 2016, https://ed.stanford.edu/news/stanford-researchers-find-students-have-trouble-judging-credibility-information-online

21. Bouygues, Helen Lee, *Fighting Fake News, Lessons from the Information Wars* (Reboot Foundation, 2019), https://reboot-foundation.org/wp-content/uploads/_docs/Fake-News-Report.pdf

22. Al-Arshani, Sarah, "False Coronavirus Information Isn't Just a Nuisance, It Could Be Deadly," *Business Insider*, August 13, 2020, https://www.businessinsider.in/international/news/false-coronavirus-information-isnt-just-a-nuisance-it-could-be-deadly-at-least-800-people-have-died-as-a-result-of-misinformation-about-the-virus-that-spread-online-during-the-first-3-months-of-the-year-study-finds-/articleshow/77515756.cms

23. "Coronavirus: False and Misleading Vaccine Claims Debunked," FR24 News, July 26, 2020, https://www.fr24news.com/a/2020/07/coronavirus-false-and-misleading-vaccine-claims-debunked.html

24. O'Neill, Saffron, Kathie Treen, and Hywel Williams, "Online Misinformation about Climate Change," *WIREs Climate Change* 11, no. 5 (September/October 2020).

Chapter 5

1. Kazi, Chandna, and Claire Hastwell, "Remote Work Productivity Study Finds Surprising Reality: 2-Year Analysis," www.greatplacetowork.com, February 10, 2021, https://www.greatplacetowork.cn/remote-work-productivity-study-finds-surprising-reality-2-year-analysis/

2. Bloom, Nicholas et al., "Does Working from Home Work? Evidence from a Chinese Experiment," *The Quarterly Journal of Economics* 130, no. 1 (February 2015).

3. Hoque, Faisal, "Ask These 3 Questions to Learn Something New at Any Career Stage," *Fast Company*, May 3, 2018, https://www.fastcompany.com/40561439/ask-these-3-questions-to-learn-something-new-at-any-career-stage

4. McKenzie, Lindsay, "Students Want Online Learning Options Post-Pandemic," Inside Higher Ed, April 27, 2021, https://www.insidehighered.com/news/2021/04/27/survey-reveals-positive-outlook-online-instruction-post-pandemic

5. Reinhardt, Andy, "Steve Jobs, 'There's Sanity Returning,'" *Businessweek*, May 25, 1998.

6. Lai, Anjalie, "Empowered Consumers Call for Sustainability Transformation," *Forbes*, January 21, 2021, https://www.forbes.com/sites/forrester/2021/01/21/empowered-consumers-call-for-sustainability-transformation/

Chapter 6

1. "Costs and Benefits," Global Workplace Analytics, https://globalworkplaceanalytics.com/resources/costs-benefits

2. "China Air Pollution Falls 10.8% because of Coronavirus Slowdown," Reuters, August 14, 2020, https://www.reuters.com/article/us-china-pollution/china-air-pollution-falls-10-8-because-of-coronavirus-slowdown-idUSKCN25A16Q

3. Townsend, Solitaire, "88% of Consumers Want You to Help Them Make a Difference," *Forbes*, November 21, 2018, https://www.forbes.com/sites/solitairetownsend/2018/11/21/consumers-want-you-to-help-them-make-a-difference

4. Hern, Alex, "Facebook and Google Announce Plans to Become Carbon Neutral," *The Guardian*, September 15, 2020, https://

www.theguardian.com/environment/2020/sep/15/facebook-and-google-announce-plans-become-carbon-neutral

5. Kirkman, Alexandra, "Inside Ikea's Ambitious Plan to Make Cheap Furniture Last Forever," *Mother Jones*, February 14, 2021, https://www.motherjones.com/environment/2021/02/ikeas-ambitious-plan-to-make-its-cheap-furniture-last-forever/

6. Outlery, "Pocket-Sized, Re-Useable Cutlery & Chopsticks for On-the-Go!" Kickstarter, https://www.kickstarter.com/projects/outlery/pocket-sized-reusable-cutlery-and-chopsticks-for-o

7. Hoque, Faisal, "Four Questions to Turn Everyone in Your Company into a Futurist," *Fast Company*, January 10, 2017, https://www.fastcompany.com/3066740/four-questions-to-turn-everyone-in-your-company-into-a-futurist

8. SA Board for People Practices, *HR's Place in the Fourth Industrial Revolution*, February 2020, https://cdn.ymaws.com/www.sabpp.co.za/resource/resmgr/siphiwe_2020/fact-sheet_february_2020.pdf

9. Dore, Debbie, "Project Managers Can Survive and Thrive in the 4IR," *Training Journal*, October 16, 2019, https://www.trainingjournal.com/articles/features/project-managers-can-survive-and-thrive-4ir

10. Djanov, Simeon, and Eva Zhang, "Startups Boom in the United States during Covid-19," Peterson Institute for International Economics, February 17, 2021, https://www.piie.com/blogs/realtime-economic-issues-watch/startups-boom-united-states-during-covid-19

11. Osborne, Shelley, *2021 Workplace Learning Trends Report* (Udemy for Business, 2021), https://info.udemy.com/rs/273-CKQ-053/images/Udemy-2021-Trends-Report.pdf

12. Palmer, Michael, "Data Is the New Oil," ANA Marketing Maestros (blog), November 3, 2006, https://ana.blogs.com/maestros/2006/11/data_is_the_new.html

13. Barnfather, Karl, "The Rise of the Data-Driven Economy Is an Opportunity for Innovators in Europe," *EU Business News*, January 13, 2021, https://www.eubusinessnews.com/the-rise-of-the-data-driven-economy-is-an-opportunity-for-innovators-in-europe/

14. Hessekiel, David, "Companies Taking a Public Stand in the Wake of George Floyd's Death," *Forbes*, June 4, 2020, https://www.forbes.com/sites/davidhessekiel/2020/06/04/companies-taking-a-public-stand-in-the-wake-of-george-floyds-death/

Chapter 7

1. World Economic Forum, *The Future of Jobs Report 2018*, September 17, 2018, https://www.weforum.org/reports/the-future-of-jobs-report-2018

2. Belcak, Austin, "Soft Skills Employers Want in 2021 [120+ examples]," Cultivated Culture, January 11, 2021, https://cultivatedculture.com/soft-skills/

3. Hoque, Faisal, "As Our Lives Become More Automated, These Are Skills You'll Need," Faisal Hoque (website), December 10, 2020, https://faisalhoque.com/2020/12/10/as-our-lives-become-more-automated-these-are-the-skills-youll-need/

4. Hoque, Faisal, "The Case for Humanities in the Era of AI, Automation, and Technology," Faisal Hoque (website), March 18, 2019, https://faisalhoque.com/2019/03/18/case-humanities-era-ai-automation-technology/

5. "Going on to Medical School, Law School, and other Graduate Schools," Philosophy, College of Liberal Arts and Sciences, University of Colorado at Denver, https://clas.ucdenver.edu/philosophy/students/going-medical-school-law-school-and-other-graduate-schools

6. Dell Technologies, Institute for the Future, *The Next Era of Human/Machines Partnerships*, 2017, https://www.iftf.org/fileadmin/user_upload/downloads/th/SR1940_IFTFforDellTechnologies_Human-Machine_070717_readerhigh-res.pdf

7. Wasik, Emily, *Bridging the Digital Divide to Engage Students in Higher Education* (London: Economist Intelligence Unit, 2020).

8. "Florida State University Reimagines Student Learning with Microsoft Teams," Customer Stories, Microsoft, March 22, 2021, https://customers.microsoft.com/en-sg/story/1351649898736060046-florida-state-university-higher-education-microsoft365-en-united-states

9. "Bioengineering Major Program," Stanford Engineering, SoE Undergrad Handbook, Stanford University, accessed October 29, 2021, https://ughb.stanford.edu/majors-minors/major-programs/bioengineering-major-program

10. "Green Chemistry," Sustainable Stanford, Stanford University, accessed October 29, 2021, https://sustainable.stanford.edu/cardinal-green/cardinal-green-labs/chemical-handling

Chapter 8

1. Tas, Jeroen et al, "Seven Visions of the Future of Healthcare," *The Daily Telegraph*, 2016, https://www.telegraph.co.uk/wellbeing/future-health/healthcare-predictions/

2. Agrawal, Mayank, Sumit Dutta, Richard Kelly, and Ingrid Millán, "COVID-19: An Inflection Point for Industry 4.0," McKinsey and Co., January 15, 2021, https://www.mckinsey.com/business-functions/operations/our-insights/covid-19-an-inflection-point-for-industry-40

3. "Portable Technologies Are Transforming Healthcare," *Healthcare Global*, May 17, 2020, https://healthcareglobal.com/technology-and-ai-3/portable-technologies-are-transforming-healthcare

4. Hoque, Faisal, "Why We Need Health-Care Business Innovation More Than Ever," *Fast Company*, October 2, 2013, https://www.fastcompany.com/3019042/why-we-need-healthcare-business-innovation-more-than-ever

5. Dolan, Brian, "iHeal Device Aims to Prevent Substance Abuse Relapses," MobiHealthNews.com, February 9, 2012, https://www.mobihealthnews. com/16272/iheal-device-aims-to-prevent-substance-abuse-relapses

6. "Number of mHealth apps available in the Apple App Store from 1st quarter 2015 to 1st quarter 2021," Statista.com, May 2021, https://www.statista.com/ statistics/779910/health-apps-available-ios-worldwide/

7. "Portable Technologies Are Transforming Healthcare," *Healthcare Global*, May 17, 2020, https://healthcareglobal.com/technology-and-ai-3/ portable-technologies-are-transforming-healthcare

8. Claflin, Jake, Justin Dimick, M.D., Kyle Sheetz, M.D., "Trends in the Adoption of Robotic Surgery for Common Surgical Procedures," Jama Network Open, January 10, 2020, https://jamanetwork.com/journals/jamanetworkopen/ fullarticle/2758472

9. "What Is a Learning Health System?" Learning Health Systems, Johns Hopkins Berman Institute of Bioethics, https://bioethics.jhu.edu/ learning-health-systems/about

10. "About Chronic Diseases," Centers for Disease Control and Prevention, last reviewed April 28, 2021, https://www.cdc.gov/chronicdisease/about/index.htm

11. "Five Things That Will Dominate the 2020s for Pharma Companies," *The Medical Futurist*, February 25, 2020, https://medicalfuturist.com/ 5-things-that-will-dominate-the-2020s-for-pharma-companies/

12. Antrim, Aislinn, "Study Finds Total Cost of Care for CAR-T, Post-Treatment Events Can Exceed $1 Million," *Pharmacy Times*, April 13, 2021, https://www. pharmacytimes.com/view/study-finds-total-cost-of-care- for-car-t-post-treatment-events-can-exceed-1-million

13. Foy, Dan, and Ratanjee Vibhas, "Four Strategies Health Care Leaders Can Use to Maximize Virtual Health Care," *American Journal of Managed Care*, June 5, 2020, https://www.ajmc.com/view/ four-strategies-health-care-leaders-can-use-to-maximize-virtual-health-care-

Chapter 9

1. Lucia, Bill, "Poll Finds Steep Drop in Satisfaction with Government in the US," Nextgov.com, February 8, 2021, https://www.nextgov.com/ cio-briefing/2021/02/poll-finds-steep-drop-satisfaction-government-us/ 171919/

2. "We Need 21st Century Responses," DFRLab, Hoque, Faisal, "Why Innovation Matters in Politics and the Public Sector," *Fast Company*, November 19, 2012, https://www.fastcompany.com/3003207/ why-innovation-matters-politics-and-public-sector., June 29, 2017, https://medium.com/dfrlab/we-need-21st-century-responses-6b7eed6750a4

3. Hoque, Faisal, "Why Innovation Matters in Politics and the Public Sector," *Fast Company*, November 19, 2012, https://www.fastcompany.com/3003207/ why-innovation-matters-politics-and-public-sector

4. Scherer, Michael, "How Obama's Data Crunchers Helped Him Win," *Time*, November 8, 2012.

5. "This AI Traffic System in Pittsburgh Has Reduced Travel Time by 25%," Mobility 21, https://mobility21.cmu.edu/this-ai-traffic-system-in-pittsburgh-has-reduced-travel-time-by-25/

6. "Here's How We're Using AI to Help Detect Misinformation," Facebook AI, November 19, 2020, https://ai.facebook.com/blog/heres-how-were-using-ai-to-help-detect-misinformation/

7. Ebi, Kevin, "How Durham, N.C. Fights Crime with Data—and Wins," Smart Cities Council, September 17, 2014, https://smartcitiescouncil.com/article/how-durham-nc-fights-crime-data-and-wins

8. Scholta, Hendrik, et al., "From One-Stop Shop to No-Stop Shop: An E-Government Stage Model," *Government Information Quarterly* 36, no. 1 (January 2019).

9. "Keolis Begins Autonomous Shuttle Trial in Gothenburg," Intelligent Transport, January 20, 2021, https://www.intelligenttransport.com/transport-news/115513/gothenburg-autonomous/

10. "How the Coca-Cola Company Enables Women Entrepreneurs," Coca-Cola, accessed October 29, 2021, https://www.coca-colacompany.com/shared-future/women-empowerment.

11. "Heineken: Launches 4 Year Barley Program in Ethiopia Together with Dutch and Ethiopian Government," MarketScreener, March 16, 2017, https://www.marketscreener.com/quote/stock/HEINEKEN-N-V-6283/news/Heineken-launches-4-year-barley-program-in-Ethiopia-together-with-Dutch-and-Ethiopian-Government-24052765/

12. "J&J Partners with India's IMTECH to Develop New Treatments for TB," Genetic Engineering & Biotechnology News, August 17, 2017, https://www.genengnews.com/topics/drug-discovery/jj-partners-with-indias-imtech-to-develop-new-treatments-for-tb/

13. Lohr, Steve, "Another Use for A.I.: Finding Millions of Unregistered Voters," *The New York Times*, November 5, 2018, https://www.nytimes.com/2018/11/05/technology/unregistered-voter-rolls.html

14. Miller, Jason, "Biden Proposal Calls Investments in Federal IT 'An Urgent National Security Issue,'" Federal News Network, January 15, 2021, https://federalnewsnetwork.com/budget/2021/01/biden-proposal-calls-investments-in-federal-it-an-urgent-national-security-issue/

Section Three

1. Saad, Lydia, "Trust in Federal Government's Competence Remains Low," Gallup, September 29, 2020, https://news.gallup.com/poll/321119/trust-federal-government-competence-remains-low.aspx

2. Jacobs, Christine et al, "The Influence of Transformational Leadership on Employee Well-Being," *Journal of Occupational and Environmental Medicine* 55, no. 7 (July 2013).

3. Chambers, John, "Cisco's John Chambers on the Digital Era," interview by Rik Kirkland, McKinsey and Co., March 18, 2016, https://www.mckinsey.com/industries/technology-media-and-telecommunications/our-insights/ciscos-john-chambers-on-the-digital-era

Chapter 10

1. Hoque, Faisal, "Good Leaders Know How to Communicate with Others— Here Are 4 Questions You Should Always Ask in Difficult Situations," *Business Insider*, July 25, 2018, https://www.businessinsider.com/emotional-intelligence-leadership-skill-7-2018

Chapter 11

1. Deloitte, *The Fourth Industrial Revolution Is Here—Are You Ready?*, 2018, https://www2.deloitte.com/content/dam/Deloitte/tr/Documents/manufacturing/Industry4-0_Are-you-ready_Report.pdf

2. Dalkiran, Seren, "The Future of Work and Leadership by Humanizing the 4IR," YouTube Video, 16:46, May 15, 2019, https://www.youtube.com/watch?v=6qnRZk3n4ug

3. Stokes, Jon, and Sue Dopson, *From Ego to Eco: Leadership in the Fourth Industrial Revolution* (Oxford: Saïd Business School, 2020), https://www.sbs.ox.ac.uk/sites/default/files/2020-03/From%20Ego%20to%20Eco%20-%20Leadership%20for%20the%20Fourth%20Industrial%20Revolution.pdf

4. Fordham, Gabelli School of Business, *Thoughtful Leadership Certification* (brochure), https://www.fordham.edu/download/downloads/id/13646/thoughtful_leadership_certification_brochure.pdf

5. Carter, Les, "12 Phrases Emotionally Intelligent People Don't Use," YouTube Video, 12:49, June 4, 2019, https://www.youtube.com/watch?v=3pPNJ61AZns

6. Hoque, Faisal, "Why Design Thinking Is Critical for a Digital Future," HackerNoon, *Medium*, May 30, 2017, https://medium.com/hackernoon/why-design-thinking-is-critical-for-a-digital-future-a724072e951d

7. Drape, Joe and Brooks Barnes, "ESPN Layoffs: The Struggling Industry Giant Sheds On-Air Talent," *The New York Times*, April 26, 2017, https://www.nytimes.com/2017/04/26/sports/espn-layoffs.html

8. Lafayette, Jon, "Disney Will Be Aggressive with Direct-to-Consumer Products," Nexttv, February 7, 2017, https://www.nexttv.com/news/disney-will-be-aggressive-direct-consumer-products-163165

9. Hoque, Faisal, "Why Design Thinking Is Critical for a Digital Future," HackerNoon, *Medium*, May 30, 2017, https://medium.com/hackernoon/why-design-thinking-is-critical-for-a-digital-future-a724072e951d

10. "Dell Technologies Research: 78% of Businesses Feel Threatened by Digital Start-Ups," Dell Technologies, October 5, 2016, https://corporate.delltechnologies.com/en-us/newsroom/unveiling-the-digital-transformation-index.htm

11. Hoque, Faisal, "Why Design Thinking Is Critical for a Digital Future," HackerNoon, *Medium*, May 30, 2017, https://medium.com/hackernoon/why-design-thinking-is-critical-for-a-digital-future-a724072e951d

12. Walker, Rob, "The Guts of a New Machine," *The New York Times Magazine*, November 30, 2003, https://www.nytimes.com/2003/11/30/magazine/the-guts-of-a-new-machine.html

13. "Design Thinking . . . What Is That?" *Fast Company*, March 20, 2006, https://www.fastcompany.com/919258/design-thinking-what

14. Hoque, Faisal, "Why Design Thinking Is Critical for a Digital Future," HackerNoon, *Medium*, May 30, 2017, https://medium.com/hackernoon/why-design-thinking-is-critical-for-a-digital-future-a724072e951d

INDEX

Electronic Registration Information Center (ERIC), 185
emotional intelligence, 197–214
  actively engaging emotions, 197
  adopting components of, 202, 204–7
  "beginner's mind," 204
  connecting systemic execution to, 213–14
  considering consequences proactively, 207
  contentment, 200
  defined, 197
  empathy, 197, 201, 207–9
  experiential learning, 200–201
  inspiration, 197
  journaling, 205
  level playing field, 201–2
  listening, 205–6
  mentoring, 207
  motivation, 204
  phrases to avoid, 222
  positive mindset, 206
  preprogramming self to adjust immediate responses, 206
  self-awareness, 204–5
  self-control, 204
  sense of commonality, 206
  shared vision, 198
  slowing down, 205
  social skills, 205
  taking responsibility for actions, 207
  trustworthiness, 201
  willingness to accept uncertainty, 199–200
empathy
  emotional intelligence, 197, 201
  leveraging opportunity through, 94
  questions to ask, 207–9
  remote work, 118
  social media, 79
  transformational leadership, 5, 43, 194
employment. *See* business and business opportunity; job skills; remote work environment. *See also* climate change
  carbon neutral and climate positive pledges, 116–19
  COVID-19 pandemic and, 52–53, 67
  educational courses related to, 147

education for remote workers, 117
  prioritization of green companies, 115–16
ERIC (Electronic Registration Information Center), 185
ESPN, 224
EU Business News, 128
Everything Connects (Hoque), 135
"expedient laziness," 78
experiential learning, 5–6, 27, 94, 104, 139, 200–201, 216, 232

F

Facebook, 17, 78–80, 116, 178
facial recognition, 28
Fast Company, 226
Federal Trade Commission, 31
Feist, Greg, 40
Fitbit, 83
5by20 Initiative, 183
Fleming, Neil D., 145
flipped classroom, 141
Florida State University, 143
Forbes.com, 103
Fordham University, 212
4D printing. *See* multidimensional printing
Fourth Industrial Revolution (4IR), 1–2, 13–33
  artificial intelligence, 25, 29–30
  climate change, 69–70
  collective mentality, 31–32
  consumer habits, 28–29
  customer service, 127–28
  data quality, 30
  disruptions caused by, 14, 17
  dividing line between automation and soft skills, 19
  drivers of, 14
  education, 27–28
  elements of, 14
  empowering population, 31
  feeling of being out of control, 93
  freelancing, 23–25
  healthcare, 25, 28, 104
  "homebody" economy, 28

patient feedback, 104
personal accountability for wellness,
104
privacy issues, 158
proactivity, 153, 157–59, 162, 163
reducing redundancies and waste, 164
remote monitoring and tracking, 153,
157, 163
response time, 152–53, 158
robotics, 160
small towns, 105–6
social media, 159
technological innovation, 152–66
telehealth services, 28, 104, 106, 158,
164–65
wearable health trackers, 25, 105, 153,
157
health insurance coverage, 50–51
Heineken, 183
Hervey, Michael, 173
Hines, Gregory, 77
"homebody" economy, 28
Hope, Ed, 159
humanitarians, 223
humanities. *See* soft skills
"Humans Wanted" (Royal Bank of Canada), 18
Humby, Clive, 128
Huq, Saleemul, 63
Hurricane Sandy, 84, 173–74

I
IBM, 164
Iger, Robert, 224
iHeal, 157
IKEA, 118–19
iLearn, 134
individual opportunity, 94–108
climate change, 103
consumer issues and habits, 103–4
consumer role, 96, 101, 103–4, 106
education, 101–2
empowerment, 3, 19, 31, 95
government, 106
healthcare, 104–5
learning potential, 99–100

workplace and employment, 96–98,
101
innovators, 223
Instagram, 78
Institute for the Future, 140
Internal Revenue Service, 176, 177
International Centre for Climate Change
and Development, 63
Internet of Things (IoT), 14–15, 122,
128, 227
"Internet of Things Is Just a Pit Stop on
the Way to Smart Dust" (Vice.com),
122
Internet's Challenge to Democracy, The
(Persily), 6

J
job skills. *See also* business and business
opportunity; soft skills
digital literacy, 18
dividing line between automation and
soft skills, 19
experiential learning, 139
global competencies, 18
green skills, 64
"human skills," 18
most important, in age of disruption,
17–18
opportunities to gain, 96–97
self management, 98
skills mobility, 18
training self-managing workers, 113
Jobs, Steve, 103, 226
Johns Hopkins University, 159
Johnson & Johnson, 183
Johnson, Lyndon B., 160
Jonas, Jeff, 185
journaling, 205
Journal of Economic Perspectives, 82
Journal of *Occupational and Environmental
Medicine*, 193
Judd, Ashley, 81

K
Kentucky Fried Chicken (KFC), 128
Kickstarter, 119

Kim Jong-Un, 83
KPMG, 21
Kurzarbeit (short work) subsidy, 46–47

L

LaBolt, Ben, 173
Lao Tzu, 41
Last Lecture, The (Pausch), 39–40
Lawyers' Committee for Civil Rights Under Law, 175
leadership. *See also* emotional intelligence; systemic execution; transformational leadership
  accepting adversity, 39–40
  achieving small goals, 41–42
  call to action, 6
  declining trust in, 192
  empathy, 5, 43
  empowerment of individuals, 3, 19, 95, 191
  guiding energy, 40–41
  increasing cynicism and mistrust, 192
  lessons for life, 39–44
  leveraging solitude, 40
  moving forward, 43–44
  mutual influence, 42–43
  transactional, 3–4, 21–22
lifelong learning, 102, 140
lift, defined, 7
Lindner, Bill, 143
Long Island Power Authority (LIPA), 173–74
Lowenkrom, Hadriana, 63

M

machine learning, 17, 141, 178
Macron, Emmanuel, 75
Madej, Carrie, 87
Maine (battleship), 74
Massachusetts Institute of Technology (MIT), 15, 31
Mayo Clinic, 159, 162–63
May, Rollo, 40
McCaughey, Betsy, 84
McGraw-Hill Companies, 142
McRaven, William Harry, 41–42
Mead, Margaret, 95

media literacy, 147–48, 184
medical errors, 154–55
Medical School Admission Requirements, 136
Medtronic, 81
mentoring, 46, 100, 141, 207
Mercer, 20
Messina, Jim, 173
metacognition, 40
#MeToo movement, 81
Microsoft, 116, 120–21
military, 180
Mills, Coleen E., 145
mindfulness, 41, 136
MindLab, 106
misinformation, 3, 73–90
  altered audio/video, 82–83
  American presidential election, 74, 82, 170, 178
  April Fool's Day, 74–75
  artificial intelligence, 178
  businesses affected by, 83–84
  climate change, 88
  COVID-19 pandemic, 76, 82, 86–88
  "death panel" rumor, 84
  distrust of established authorities, 76
  distrust of media, 76–77
  email scams, 85
  entertainment-oriented fake news, 83
  "expedient laziness," 78
  Fourth Industrial Revolution, 88
  French presidential election, 75
  global costs of, 83–84
  government policies against, 86
  growth in, 82
  healthcare, 84, 163
  Hurricane Sandy, 84
  media literacy, 147–48
  opportunities afforded by, 7
  "reactance," 76
  social media, 3, 77
  Spanish-American War, 74
  threat to democracy, 6
  young people, 86
MIT (Massachusetts Institute of Technology), 15, 31
multidimensional printing, 1, 14, 16–17
Musk, Elon, 19

U

United Nations, 58
University of Baltimore, 83
University of California, 48, 69
University of Colorado, 65
University of Maryland, 48
University of Massachusetts Medical
   School, 157
University of Oxford, 17, 212
University of Southern California, 20
University of Toronto, 164
Upwork, 24
US Citizenship and Immigration Services,
   180
US Department of Defense, 180
US Department of Transportation, 15
US National Park Service, 60

V

VARK learning styles, 145–46
Varshavski, Mike, 159
Verified Voting, 175
Vice.com, 122
virtual reality, 146
voter ID laws, 175

W

Wall Street Journal, 77
wearable health trackers, 25, 105, 153,
   157
"We Working," 129
WIREs Climate Change, 88
work-life balance, 23, 101
workplace. *See* business and business
   opportunity; job skills; remote work
World Economic Forum (WEF), 2, 17,
   57–58, 78–79, 135, 172, 181–82,
   186

Y

Yale University, 197
You Can Do Anything (Anders), 18
YouTube, 130, 159

Z

Zoom, 20, 26, 27, 45–46, 102, 117,
   145–46

ABOUT THE AUTHORS

FAISAL HOQUE is an accomplished entrepreneur, senior executive, author, thought leader, public speaker, and advisor to management teams and boards of directors with more than 25 years of cross-industry success. He is the founder of SHADOKA, NextChapter, and other companies. They focus on enabling sustainable and transformational changes.

Throughout his career, he has developed over 20 commercial business and technology platforms and worked with public- and private-sector giants such as US Department of Defense (DoD), GE, MasterCard, American Express, Northrop Grumman, CACI, PepsiCo, IBM, Home Depot, Netscape, Infosys, French Social Security Services, Gartner, Cambridge Technology Partners, JP Morgan Chase, CSC, and others. What sets Faisal apart is the unique position and perspective he has always maintained, which is grounded in hardcore technology with deep roots in leading-edge management science.

As a thought leader, he has authored a number of books on leadership, innovation, mindfulness, resilience, organizational transformation, and entrepreneurship, including *Everything Connects—How to Transform* and

Lead in the Age of Creativity, Innovation and Sustainability. His work has appeared in *Fast Company, Business Insider, Wall Street Journal, Business-Week, Fox, CBS, Financial Times, Mergers & Acquisitions, Forbes, Leadership Excellence,* and *Huffington Post,* among other publications.

American Management Association (AMA) named him one of the Leaders to Watch. The editors of Ziff-Davis Enterprise named him one of the Top 100 Most Influential People in Technology alongside leading entrepreneurs such as Steve Jobs, Bill Gates, Michael Dell, Larry Page, and others. Trust Across America-Trust Around the World (TAA-TWA) named him one of the Top 100 Thought Leaders alongside global leaders such as Bill George, Doug Conant, Howard Schultz, and others.

His broad areas of expertise include innovation, leadership, management, sustainable growth, transformation, strategy, governance, M&A, frameworks, and digital platforms. He holds a strong belief that it is through knowledge sharing that we may provide the greatest clarity on how to improve our collective future. As a globetrotter, he is passionate about nature, people, culture, music, and design, and he loves to cook.

For more info, visit www.faisalhoque.com or follow him on Twitter @faisal_hoque and on LinkedIn: www.linkedin.com/in/faisalhoque/.

Photo Credit: Jeff Wuorio

JEFF WUORIO has written more than 30 books covering entrepreneurship, leadership, progressive workplaces, and other similar subjects. His work has also appeared in *Time, Business Week, Money Magazine, Fortune, USA Today,* and many other publications and websites. He lives and works in Maine.

Photo Credit: Shelley Moench-Kelly

SHELLEY MOENCH-KELLY is a New York–based writer with more than 3,500 published articles and blogs for freelance clients that include Google, L'Oréal Paris, Paramount Studios, Warner Bros., Marvel Comics, The Week. com, Prevention.com, LendingUSA.com, Mamapedia.com, and Radisson Blu Hotels. She is a longtime member of the Association of Ghostwriters, the Freelancers Union, and The Author's Guild. Her latest book, *Here's Your Pill, Kitten!* is available on Amazon.